Python Programming for Beginners:
Go from Novice to Ninja with this Stress-Free Guide to Confident Python Programming Featuring Clear Explanations and Hands-on Examples

Glenn Haertlein

:

DEDICATION

Dedicated first and foremost to my Lord and Savior Jesus Christ by whose grace I have a place prepared for me in Heaven (John 14:2, 6), and to my wife who is the love of my life and my best friend on earth.

Copyright © 2023 Glenn Haertlein

ISBN: 9798874242077

DISCLAIMER

Please note the information contained within this document is for educational and entertainment purposes only. All effort has been exercised to present accurate, up-to-date, and reliable, complete information. No warranties of any kind are declared or implied. Readers acknowledge that the author is not engaging in the rendering of legal, financial, medical, or professional advice. The content within this book has been derived from various sources. Please consult a licensed professional before attempting any techniques outlined in this book.

By reading this document, the reader agrees that under no circumstances is the author responsible for any losses, direct or indirect, which are incurred as a result of the use of information contained within this document, including, but not limited to errors, omissions, or inaccuracies.

CONTENTS

Python is known for its readability, simplicity, and ease of use. Because of these and several other characteristics, it is a great programming language for beginners, but don't let those features fool you into thinking Python is somehow second-rate. It's exactly because of those features and its rapid development capabilities that it has an impressive resumé. Here is a short list of companies that use Python:

Reddit, one of the world's largest social media and discussion platforms, started off using Common Lisp and later migrated to Python because of its readability and ease of use.

Pinterest, an image-sharing and social media platform, uses Python extensively.

Quora is a question-and-answer platform founded by former Facebook employees and of all the options out there, they chose Python as their development platform of choice.

Spotify, a music streaming company, uses Python for several things including data analysis and parts of its backend infrastructure. The same holds true for **Uber,** the ride-sharing company.

Survey Monkey, a company specializing in survey development and data collection started out with Python and continues to use it for internal tools and scripts as well as Django, Python's high-level web framework.

A surprise on this list of clients is **NASA**. Technically it is not a company but to have it as part of your list of clients is impressive. NASA uses Python for scientific and computational tasks, data analysis, and simulations.

So, if you're new to programming, trying to change career paths and move into the tech sector, or just looking to add to your skill set, learning Python is a worthy investment.

What is This Book About Python Going to Do for You?

I have three overarching goals in mind for you in this book.

Goal #1 – A strong foundation. A strong foundation in Python programming is fundamental to helping you build confidence in your programming abilities. My goal is to give you something you can continue to build on beyond the pages of this book. As part of that strong foundation, we will work to help you master fundamental concepts and syntax.

If you've ever learned a foreign language, you know that you often start by learning the alphabet, and then you progress to a few vocabulary words. From there you move on to sentence structure so that you can convey ideas. Learning a programming language is a little like that, but our goal will be to make you *fluent* in Python. So that you can be confident in it. Along the way, you'll also learn building blocks that are common to most programming languages so that you can feel confident in extending your programming knowledge into other coding languages.

Goal #2 – Learning through practical application. The only way to learn any programming language is to just start using it. This book is built around programming projects that address practical scenarios, and solving common problems to help you apply the Python concepts you are learning. So, by the time you're done, you'll have some practical programming experience under your belt.

Goal #3 – Skill building. This is related to the previous goal but goes beyond just *knowing how* to apply it and *why*. Again, this is so that you can continue to explore Python (and other programming languages) independently.

Bonus: There are two coding projects that we will build throughout this book: A GUI-based weather app and a web-based weather app that We'll deploy online. So, not only will you learn Python, but you'll also have a couple of apps to show for it!

Here's what you'll learn:
Chapter One: Python Essentials

- You'll learn why Python is a great language for beginners as well as a great choice for helping to enhance your career and skill set.

- You'll be shown how to set up Python on your machine whether your OS is Windows, Linux, or macOS.

- You'll write your first Python script.

- You'll also start on your first standalone app: A GUI-based weather application.

Chapter Two: Diving Deeper into Python.

- We'll dive deeper into operators and expressions.

- You'll see what they are, how to use them, and why.

- We'll explore loops and iteration, concepts that are fundamental to a strong foundation in programming.

- You'll take what you've learned here to continue working on the weather app.

Chapter Three: Building Functions.

- You'll learn how to define functions according to proper Python standards.

- We'll explain parameters and arguments, and how to use them.

- You'll also learn how to create and use return statements.

- We'll also continue to build on your knowledge of correct Python syntax so that your code is compliant with Python standards and looks clean, clear, and professional.

- We'll apply what you've learned here to define the function in the GUI-based weather app.

Chapter Four: Data Structures in Python.

- Lists and tuples, what they are, and how to use them.
- Dictionaries and sets, how they compare to lists and tuples, and how they can help organize and retrieve data from complex data sets.

- How to work with files, including writing a script to manage files.
- We'll also finish developing the GUI weather app.

Chapter Five: Python and Object-Oriented Programming.

- We'll cover what OOP is.

- We'll look at "is a" and "has a" relationships.

- We'll also build a car class as a hands-on demonstration of OOP.

Chapter Six: Debugging and Troubleshooting.

- Here we'll cover common Python errors and how to correct them.

- We'll learn how to do systematic troubleshooting and about the tools you can use to isolate and solve problems within your code.

- And we'll go over best practices to minimize coding errors.

Chapter Seven: Web Development with Python.

- We'll discuss the most common ways to deploy your Python scripts and look at the pros and cons of each.

- We'll create a command line version of the weather app and how we can use and interpret JSON data.

- We'll then use our command-line app to build a web-based version of our weather app and deploy that to the web.

- As part of that journey, we'll also cover some GitHub basics.

Chapter Eight: Data Analysis and Visualization with Python.

- We'll use a sample data set to do some simple data analysis.

- From there, we'll use Python's data visualization tools to create a bar chart and pie chart to tell our data's story visually.

Chapter Nine: Python in the Real Word.

- We'll continue our journey into Python by doing several hands-on automation scripts by creating the following:

  o A file copying script that does a simple copy-and-paste action that you can easily modify to do other file-handling tasks.

  o A folder organization script that will help organize cluttered files into subfolders.

  o A bulk mailer that reads a CSV file and generates personalized emails.

Chapter Ten: Database Basics and Python Integration

- Chapter 10 focuses on using Python with databases.
  o We'll go over basic SQL actions known collectively as CRUD.
  o We'll discuss different kinds of databases, and what DB platforms work well with Python.
  o We'll learn how to connect Python to a database.
  o We'll take this knowledge and connect to a MySQL database where we'll write modules to handle each of the CRUD actions and use them to manipulate data.

1 PYTHON ESSENTIALS

D id you know? A Stack Overflow survey showed that Python is the language of choice for 66% of data scientists and 41% of machine learning engineers. Python's versatility and powerful libraries are the driving force behind this preference.

Section 1: Python Basics

Understanding Python's Simplicity and Versatility

Okay, so we've mentioned this several times in this book so far. Time to put some proof behind the claim. What do we mean when we say, "Python is simple and versatile?"

It is Built Around Human Readable Code

One thing you'll notice about Python code from the start is that it reads like plain English. It's almost like pseudo-code, making it a natural choice for beginners, and because it prioritizes readability, it's a fan favorite amongst developers as well because it results in clean and elegant code. If you've ever seen or written Java code you know it's a great language, a classic one, but if you've ever had to jump into the middle of someone else's Java code (or even your *own*), you know it can sometimes take a while to decipher what the code is about and what the coder was thinking when they wrote it. While that can be true of any code, Python has a natural readability that makes it much easier to determine what the code is about and what it's supposed to do.

Why is this important?

Easy accessibility for beginners. Python speaks "human," meaning anyone, even people with no programming background, can learn it. It's not like you're seeing a bunch of words and terms on the screen that make little sense.

Easier collaboration. As already mentioned, when it comes to some coding languages it can be hard to jump into the middle of someone else's code and decipher what's going on. Python's plain-spoken readability makes it easy to grasp one another's code, making it easier to collaborate on projects even if you're new to the team.

It is Versatile Across Industries

Python is not purpose-built for any specific industry. In other words, it's not just for the scientific computation and mathematics community, and it's not just for web development. It's cross-cultural as programming languages go.

Some of the industries where Python enjoys widespread acceptance include:

- Web development

- Data science and machine learning

- Automation

- Scientific computing (Computational science)

- Game development

Why is this important?

Wide range of opportunities. Because Python is not locked into one industry and is easily adaptable, learning Python opens a wide range of opportunities for you as a Python programmer. With that skill set, you can easily transition from one industry to another.

Cross-domain solutions. Because Python can easily transition between industries, it can also provide solutions to many different industries. It also plays well with others, meaning it can be combined with other platforms, making it highly scalable.

It is a High-level Language

A high-level language is a computing language that "abstracts" many of the lower-level details such as memory management. Think of it this way: You don't have to think about keeping your heart rate at a healthy level. Your brain handles that automatically so you can do more important stuff like worry about how you're going to pay this month's electric bill.

Why is this important?

You can focus on problem-solving. Because Python allows you to do programming at a high level, you can focus on problem-solving a specific task without having to worry about things like memory leaks, or how your code is going to communicate with your computer's hardware. Python does all that for you seamlessly.

It has a Large, Active Community

When it comes to Python, you are never alone on your development journey. Because it is open-sourced, tools, libraries, forums, and resources to answer your Python problems are everywhere.

Why is this important?

Abundance of resources. Whether you're going to a forum like Stack Overflow, or tapping into open-source libraries like GitHub, Python's community of developers provides ample resources to draw from.

Setting Up Python

If you're going to start using Python, you need to have it set up on your machine. Python is available across many platforms. For this book, I'll give you instructions for Windows, macOS, and Linux. Other than the differences in how to set up Python on your OS, all other Python steps you learn will apply to you regardless of your OS.

As of this writing, there are two versions of Python available: Version 2 and Version 3. Version 2 is the legacy version and is no longer actively supported. Please use Version 3 as this is the one actively supported and the one we'll be using in this book.

Installation

Just in case, it's good to check if you have any versions of Python on your machine now. To do this, go to the command prompt on your machine. In Windows, if you type *CMD* in the search section of your taskbar, and press ENTER, you'll see the command prompt. In macOS and Linux, the command prompt is referred to as "the terminal."

In the command prompt, type *python --version*

That's "python", followed by a space, two dashes, and the word "version" right after the dashes. Now press ENTER. If you do not have Python installed, you'll see a "Python not found error." If you *do* have Python installed, make a note of the version. You might need to upgrade your Python version unless you have a compelling need not to.

You Windows users might notice that if you just type "python" at the command prompt and press ENTER, the Windows store will open. While you can install Python that way, I recommend that you *do not*. Follow the instructions below instead.

Installation steps for Windows

Step 1: In your browser, navigate to python.org. It will take you to a site that looks like this:

When you hover over the **Downloads** menu, the site will attempt to show you the version best suited to your OS. If for some reason, that is incorrect, click on **All releases**, or on the platform that matches what you are using. Be sure to download the stable release version of Python, not any of the beta versions. This book will be using the latest available stable release version at the time of this writing.

Step 2: Once you have downloaded the Python installation file, open it, and follow the prompts. You'll see a screen like this:

Step 3: Be sure to put a checkmark in the two boxes at the bottom of the install screen *before* proceeding. "Admin privileges" will make sure you can install the software without any user issues. The "Add to path" option will make sure that your OS knows where to find the executables for the Python software.

Step 4: Click the "Customize installation" option on the installation screen.

- Leave the "Optional Features" as they are and then click "Next."

- In the "Advanced Options" section, put a checkmark where it says "Install Python X.XX for <u>all</u> users" where the X's represent your version number.

- The program will install to the default path on your machine. Only change this if you have good reason to do so.

- Click "Install."

On Windows you may be asked if you want to proceed with the installation, just choose "Yes."

Installation steps for macOS
Step 1: Open your terminal.

Step 2: Install Homebrew if you don't already have it.

```
You can install Homebrew by running `/bin/bash -c
"$(curl -fsSL
https://raw.githubusercontent.com/Homebrew/install/maste
r/install.sh)"`
```

Step 3: Install Python 3 by running `brew install python3`

Installation for Linux (applies to Ubuntu and Debian)
Step 1: Open your terminal.

Step 2: Use this command to update your package list: `sudo apt update`

Step 3: Install Python 3 by running: `sudo apt install python3`

Check your installation
To make sure Python installed correctly, go to the

command prompt (or terminal and again run this command:
python --version

You should see a prompt showing you what version of Python you have installed.

Test Run
From the command prompt (terminal) run this command:

Python

You should see another prompt known as the Python interpreter appear in the command/terminal window. Now type this and then press ENTER:

print("Hello, Python!")

It should respond with: Hello, Python!

To get out of the Python interpreter type exit() or press CRL+Z and then press ENTER. That will return control to your command/terminal window.

Development Environment (IDEs)

While you can create Python programs using a simple text editor, most developers prefer to use what is called an Integrated Development Environment or IDE. IDE's can help you with syntax, bug fixing, coding hints, and more. Popular Python IDEs include Python and Jupyter Notebook. However, I prefer to use Visual Studio Code because it can support multiple coding languages, it's popular among developers in general and provides a more robust coding environment.

Installing Visual Studio Code

Step 1: Visit Visual Studio Code's website:

(https://code.visualstudio.com/)

Step 2: Download the version that applies to your operating system.

Step 3: Open VSCode and optionally install the Python extensions. For complete instructions for this step, go to this link:

https://code.visualstudio.com/docs/python/python-tutorial

Throughout this book, we will be doing our coding examples in VSCode. However, you are free to use whichever IDE you prefer. And now that you have completed your setup, you're ready to get started on your Python programming journey! Let's Go!

Your First Python Program!

If you've come this far, that means you've already set up Python on your machine. Congratulations! I think that's the hardest part of the whole process. Now the fun begins! So, let's get started on the classic "Hello, world!" program. For most programming languages, the "Hello, world!" program is the rite of passage into any new coding language you embark upon. By the time you are done with this section, you'll have written and executed your first Python program!

Launch Your Code Editor

If you installed VSCode, just open that and create a new file using these steps:

- Click **File → New File (CTRL+ALT+WIN+N).**

- When prompted, give the file a name like "hello.py". It *must* have the ".py" extension.

- Save it.

Write Your First Piece of Python Code
Just type this into the code editor:

```
print("Hello, World!")
```

Running Your Code
First, be sure to save your file if you have not already. In VSCode any file(s) that have not been saved yet will have a dot next to the file name.

Second, open a terminal window in VSCode. To do that, go to the top menu and click *Terminal >> New Terminal*. (CTRL+ `) For the keyboard shortcut, the backtick (`) is usually located under the ESC key. The terminal screen will appear at the bottom of the VSCode window.

Third, navigate to where you saved your file. If you don't remember where that was, look just above your first line of code in the code editor. You'll see the path spelled out for you. Navigate to that path in the terminal window.

For Windows:

cd path\to\your\file

For macOS and Linux:

cd /path/to/your/file

("CD" = change directory or change disk)

Fourth, type python hello.py without the quotes. If everything runs right, you should see "Hello, World!" in the terminal.

```
PROBLEMS    OUTPUT    DEBUG CONSOLE    TERMINAL

PS C:\Users\htack\OneDrive\Programming\python> python hello.py
Hello, World!
PS C:\Users\htack\OneDrive\Programming\python> █
```

💡	In VSCode, if you want to clear the screen, just type "clear" without the quotes and press ENTER.
💡	If you want to reuse a command you just typed, use the up or down arrow to cycle through recent commands.
	Tip icons created by Pixel Perfect - Flaticon

By the way, congratulations! You just created your first piece of Python code! You are a Python coder now! (Too late. You can't go back.)

Now let's take a close look at the code you just wrote.

Understanding the Code
```
print("Hello, World!")
```

- This command is using a function and a variable.

- When you call a function, you always end it with a pair of parentheses ("parens" for short), even if you don't put anything in them. This is how Python understands you're calling a function and not just randomly typing in a word.

- Inside the parens of the print() function, we passed in a string variable. A variable is a value that can change. They are passed to methods and functions to be acted upon. In our example, we passed the string variable "Hello, World!" to the print() function so it could show that on the screen. Because it is a *variable*, we could have put any string we wanted. For example, we could have put, "I miss Tom Brady!" and our code would have said that instead. What is important to note is that *string variables must always be surrounded by quotes.*

- We did not use this in our code, but in Python, if you want to add a comment to your code, you would precede your comment with a # (hash/pound sign). Don't confuse that with a hashtag you might use on social media. Not the same thing! When Python sees a #, it knows it's not supposed to process that line as code. It is just a comment for the sake of the programmers looking at it.

- Below is an example of a code comment.

As you can see, line one only appears in my code. It does not appear in the output.

Why are comments important?
Comments are important because they are a good way to document your code to explain what you were doing and why when you wrote the code. This way, when you or someone else comes back to it, you have your notes to jog your memory.

Section 2: Python Variables and Data Types

Variables

Variables are a crucial part of programming. They make your code dynamic. In the "Hello, World!" example, we used a variable in the print() function. Thanks to variables, the print() function can do more than just say "Hello, World!" It can say all kinds of things.

In Python (and most other coding languages), a variable is a container for storing data. Let's say you had a recycling station with four receptacles. The first was labeled "Glass". The second was labeled "Plastic." The third was labeled "Paper." And the fourth was labeled "Aluminum cans." Now it's recycling day and you're the guy who has to take everything to the recycling plant. In an ideal world, each of your containers would only contain what the label said. Those were the variables. But we don't live in an ideal world. Not everybody follows the rules, and it would not be surprising to you as the recycling guy to find stuff in the wrong containers or to find stuff that didn't even belong in the containers (concrete blocks, 2x4s, etc.)

In the coding world, it's not so chaotic. Variables have *types*.

Data Types

Data types determine what kind of data a variable can hold. If a variable is declared to be of type string, it can only have strings (or characters) in it. Data types are crucial in programming languages because the data type of a variable determines what kinds of operations can be performed with that variable. For example, if I had a variable called "Y" and gave it a data type of string and then stored the string "dog" inside it, that would be fine. But then if I tried to multiply variable Y by 3, I'd get some kind of data type error because you can't multiply "dog" * 3. It makes no sense. Variables all have data types, and those types must be respected.

This list shown here is just to give you an overview. Don't get too bogged down trying to figure everything out here. Things will make more sense as we progress through the book.

- **Integers (int):** These are whole numbers both positive and negative. (Ex.: 0, -1, 23)

- **Floating-point Numbers (float):** These are numbers both positive and negative with decimals. (Ex.: 0.34, 3.14, -1.72)

- **Strings (str):** These are sequences of characters. Strings can be enclosed with single ("), double ("), or triple quotes (""", or """). (Ex.: "dog", "12345", "jumping the shark"). When you enclose a number with quotes, it becomes a *string representation* of that number, not the value. I can add 7+7. I cannot add "7" + 7.

- **Boolean (bool):** Booleans represent true or false values. They are crucial to conditional statements.

- **Lists:** These are *ordered* collections of elements. This means items in a list will each have an index indicating their position in the list. You can add or remove items from a list as needed. Lists can be of various data types and are enclosed in square brackets ([ ]). For example, [5,6,7] and ["eggs", "bacon", "toast"] are both lists. The first one is an integer list and the second is a string list.

- **Tuples:** These are like lists except they are immutable, meaning you cannot add/remove members once the tuple has been declared. They are used for fixed collections of data. For example, you might have a string tuple that contains the names of the planets in our solar system. That is unchangeable – unless the scientific community demotes yet another planet from the list. (Pluto forever, my brothers and sisters!) Tuples are enclosed in parentheses. Example: (1,2,3)

- **Dictionaries (dict):** These are *unordered* collections of key-value pairs. Each value in the dictionary is connected to a unique key. You would use the key to retrieve the value from the dictionary. Dictionaries are defined with curly braces and colons like this: {"object" : "ball", "color" : "blue", "material" : "plastic"} So if I were using this dictionary, and I wanted to know what kind of object is in it, I could retrieve the object key and find out it is a ball.

- **Sets:** Sets are also *unordered* collections of unique elements. They are also declared using curly braces, but they contain no keys. Example: {1, 2, 3}

- **NoneType (None):** First, note that the abbreviated form of this type is *capitalized*. It is "None," not "none." None is used to represent the *absence* of a value. In Python, it is used to indicate a missing or undefined value.

Complex Numbers (complex): These consist of a real part and an imaginary part. For example, in 2 + 3j, 2 is the real part and 3 is the imaginary part.

With these essential data types, Python can handle a wide range of data from the simple to the complex.

Integers

As we mentioned above, integers are *whole* numbers, meaning they are numbers with no decimals. Integers can be negative or positive. So, numbers like 12, -7, 0, and 115 are all integers. Integers are used often in calculations and as indexes in things like lists.

Floats

Floats are numbers that have decimals. These are also referred to as "floating point" numbers. It's like calling snap beans *haricot vert*. Same thing, just a different name. Floats can be positive or negative. So, numbers like 3.14, -2.6, and 0.1 are all floats. Floats are typically used when greater precision is needed.

Strings (str)

Strings and string manipulation are an integral part of the Python programming language. We use strings to communicate with our users to explain results or provide feedback. As mentioned earlier, strings are surrounded by single ("), double (""), or triple quotes ("' or """"). If you try to declare a string and forget to enclose it in quotes, Python will throw an error message at run time. If you're using a code editor like VSCode, your editor will flag it as a syntax error.

Here are some common string operations:

Concatenation (+)

Concatenation is when you take two (or more) strings and connect them using the "+" operator. Here is an example:

```python
string1 = "Hello, "
string2 = "Python!"
combined_string = string1 + string2  # Result: "Hello, Python!"
print(combined_string)
```

String Length (len( ))

The len() function will return the length of a string. Have a look at this example.

```python
text = "Python is awesome!"
length = len(text)
print(str(length)) # result = 18
```

The length of our text from start to finish is 18 characters. This includes spaces. If our string had leading or trailing spaces, they would also have been included in the length count.

Indexing and Slicing

Strings are strings of characters, they also have indexes. In Python, indexes start with 0 (zero). So, to get the first character of a string you would request the character at index 0. Here is an example:

```
11    text = "Python is awesome!"
12    first_character = text[0]   # Result: 'P'
13    substring = text[7:18]   # Result: 'is awesome!'
14    print('length: ' + str(len(text)))
15    print('first_character: ' + first_character)
16    print('substring: ' + substring)
```

On line 12 I asked for the first character of the string and so I wrote text[0]. If I had asked for text[1], I would have received the *second* character in the string because indexes start with 0 in Python.

On line 13 when I wanted a substring, I asked to start with the character right after the space following "Python". It's the 8th character but because of the 0-based index, I requested character 7. To get the rest of the string, I just entered 18 after the colon. I could have entered the len( ) function there and gotten the same result.

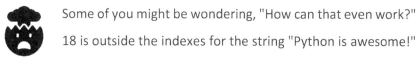 Some of you might be wondering, "How can that even work?" 18 is outside the indexes for the string "Python is awesome!" The last character is at index 17. True. But you have to consider how the substring() function in Python works. The end of the substring statement is not included in the substring. (This is true of languages like Visual Basic as well.) So, to get all the ending characters,

you have to enter a number one greater than the index of the last character.

(See https://www.freecodecamp.org/news/how-to-substring-a-string-in-python/ for more information.)

Mind-blowing icons created by Nurlaili - Flaticon

String Methods
Python's string methods allow you to manipulate and format strings. Consider these examples:

```
text = "Hello, Python!"
uppercase_text = text.upper()  # Result: 'HELLO, PYTHON!'
lowercase_text = text.lower()  # Result: 'hello, python!'
replaced_text = text.replace("Python", "World")  # Result: 'Hello, World!'
```

Uppercase and lowercase are self-explanatory. They change the case of the given string.

Replace will replace the text in a given string with a new string. In our example, we are replacing "Python" in "Hello, Python" with the word "World" to get "Hello, World!"

Quick Recap
Using and manipulating strings and numbers is a fundamental part of using Python. It's foundational to becoming proficient in this language. The more you practice, the better you'll get at it. Don't be discouraged if some things don't seem to make sense at first. The more you use it and learn from your mistakes, the more you'll gain.

Type Conversion

Sometimes you need to combine types. Python allows you to convert from float to int and vice versa. I know a lot is going on in the sample code below, but for now, just enter it into your preferred code editor (without the line numbers). Save it as *TypeConversionExample.py* and run it.

```
TypeConversionExample.py > ...
1    integer_number = 5
2    float_number = float(integer_number)   # Convert to float
3    result = integer_number / float_number
4    print("integer_number: " + str(integer_number))
5    print("float_number: " + str(float_number))
6    print("result: " + str(result))
```

Code Explanation

Line 1: This is a comment showing what this code is about.

Line 2: This declares a variable called "integer_number." Because it has no decimal value, Python assumes it is an int. It does not need to be explicitly declared as an int.

Line 3: This declares the variable "float_number". Because we want Python to treat this as a float, we have to "cast" it as a float like this: float(integer_number). This tells Python to take our integer and treat it as a float for our "float_number" variable.

Line 4: This is taking our int and dividing it by our float.

Line 5: This gave you the whole number 5.

Line 6: This gave you the float number 5.0 because floats always have decimals.

27

Line 7: This gave you a *float* result. Why? Because when you do operations where types are mixed, the result will be *promoted* to the higher type. Integers are a basic type. Floats are a higher-order type (for lack of a better term).

In lines 5-7 you may have noticed this syntax in the print() function:

```
str(variable_name)
```

This is because the print() function can only take string parameters. Before you can use it to print out numeric results, the result must be converted to a string. So, what you're seeing is another data type conversion but this time from a numeric data type to a string data type. You might also have noticed a plus (+) sign between the string statement and the str(variable_name) notation. This is not adding the strings. This is called "concatenation," where several string results are connected to one another.

Just for Fun
Let's try switching some things up. Try this in your code editor and run it:

```
float_number = 5.9

integer_number = int(float_number)

print("float_number: " + str(float_number))

print("integer_number: " + str(integer_number))
```

What did the integer value become? You might have expected it to round up to 6. Instead, it just removed the decimal part and gave back 5. When you're doing type conversions, choose wisely and consider if the conversion is going to cause you to lose precision in the results and whether that will impact what you are expecting.

Basic Numeric Operations

Python has a wide range of numeric operations it can perform. That's one of the reasons it is so popular in the science and mathematics communities. Below is a table of the most commonly used Python operators.

+	Addition
-	Subtraction
*	Multiplication
/	Division
//	Floor (or integer) Division
%	Modulo (or Remainder). Returns the remainder of the numbers being divided.
**	Exponentiation

The code samples below demonstrate these operators in action. To try these for yourself, create a file called *BasicOps.py* in your code editor and enter the code below:

```
1    # Basic Numeric Operations
2    a = 6
3    b = 4
4
```

```
5    # Addition
6    addition_result = a + b
7    print('Addition: a + b = ' + str(addition_result))
8
```

```
9    # Subtraction
10   subtraction_result = a - b
11   print('Subtraction: a - b = ' + str(subtraction_result))
12
```

```
13   # Multiplication
14   multiplication_result = a * b
15   print('Multiplication: a * b = ' + str(multiplication_result))
16
```

```
17   # Division
18   division_result = a / b
19   print('Division: a / b = ' + str(division_result))
20
```

```
21   # Integer Division (floor division)
22   floor_division_result = a // b
23   print('Floor Division: a // b = ' + str(floor_division_result))
24
```

```
28
29   # Exponentiation
30   exponentiation_result = a ** b  # Result: 25
31   print('Exponentiation: a ** b = ' + str(exponentiation_result))
```

Code Explanation

Lines 1-8: These are self-explanatory and the operators used are common math operators.

Lines 9-11: Here just note that the operator for multiplication in Python (and most coding languages) is * (asterisk). Also, because we are using integer values, we are getting an integer result.

Lines 12-14: You might find this a little unexpected. We are dividing integers, but we are getting a decimal result. (1.5) This is the default behavior for Python 3.

Lines 15-17: This is integer (or floor) division and the operator is double forward slashes (//). When you divide using this operator, you will only get the whole number result even if there is a remainder, Hence the result, 1.

"In Python, we can perform floor division (also sometimes known as integer division) using the // operator. This operator will divide the first argument by the second and round the result down to the nearest whole number, making it equivalent to the math.floor() function." (Python Double Slash (//) Operator: Floor Division – LearnDataSCI, n.d.)

Lines 18-20: This is modulo or remainder division. The "mod" operator is the percent sign (%). This operation returns the remainder of two numbers when divided. For example, if you have a set of numbers and you want all the even ones, you could iterate through the set dividing each number by % 2 (mod 2) and then extract only the numbers where x

% 2 = 0 where "x" is one of the numbers from the set. 12 % 2 (12 mod 2), for example, would have no remainder, so it would be one of the numbers extracted.

Lines 21-23: If you need to apply an exponent to a number, the exponentiation operator is **. In our example, we took 6 to the power of 4 so Python did this with 6 ** 4 and gave us the result of 1296.

Calling Functions vs. Calling Methods

One more thing before we go on to the coding practice for this section, and that's calling functions vs. calling methods. You've already seen the print( ) function several times. You also saw the .upper( ) and .lower( ) methods in action. There is a significant difference in how functions and methods are called. Functions can be called from anywhere. Methods, however, must be attached to an object or a class. If you look at the ".upper( )" method above, you'll see that it is *attached* to the text object we created. The text object in our example is a String data type. I cannot call "upper" from out of nowhere. I have to have an object to attach it to and I have to use "dot notation" to use it. Notice in the code that it was "text.upper()," not just "upper." If you were reading that code aloud, you read it as "text dot upper." That "dot" is what attaches the method to a class/object. To put it another way, a method cannot act independently. A function, however, can be called from anywhere. You've seen that in all the print() function calls we've made so far. It was not 'some_object dot print." It was just print(TEXT).

"In Python, methods and functions have similar purposes but differ in important ways. Functions are independent blocks of code that can be called from anywhere, while methods are tied to objects or classes and need an object or class instance to be invoked. Functions promote code reusability, while methods offer behavior specific to objects. Functions are called by name, while methods are accessed using dot notation. Understanding these distinctions is crucial for writing organized, modular code in Python and harnessing the full power of methods and functions in various programming scenarios. " (Singh & Singh, 2023)

The more we try out code and experiment with methods and functions, the more this will make sense. You're doing great! Keep reading!

Coding Practice for Section 2

Answers to the coding practices will be at the back of the book. Try not to peek until you're sure your code works. It doesn't matter if your solution does not look just like mine. What matters is that solutions work and work consistently.

Add 2 Numbers

Declare two variables and make them floats.

Sum the numbers.

Display them in the terminal using the print() method.

EXTRA: Use the input() function to get numbers from your user. The input function looks like this: `input("Enter your first number: ")`

Hint: Put the input function inside your float function.

Manipulate a String
Take a sentence and get its length.

Display the length in the terminal.

Convert the sentence to uppercase and display that.

EXTRA: Use the input() function to get a sentence from the user.

Concatenate Strings to Make a Greeting
Make two string variables. Label one first_name and the other last_name.

Concatenate those into a variable called full_name.

Make a greeting variable called greeting.

Concatenate everything to print a message that says: "Greetings, [full_name]. Welcome to Python!"

EXTRA: Use the `input()` method to get the first and last name of the user for your greeting message.

As I said above, if you tried these and got the right outcome, great! Your solution does not have to look exactly like the ones in the answer key, but as we'll see in the next section, some things in Python really do matter!

Section 3: Python Syntax

Python's Unique Indentation Requirements

Indentation Matters
Unlike some programming languages that use braces or other symbols to structure their code, Python relies on a strict set of indentation rules. For

Python, correct indentation is crucial for defining blocks of code such as loops, conditionals, and functions. While those coming from other programming languages may find that a bit unusual if not sometimes frustrating, it's Python's adherence to those rules that make it a user-friendly and easily readable language.

Correct Python Example:
This is an example of an if/else statement. In Python, the main part of the statement goes on its own line. If there is a block after it, the main clause ends in a colon and the block is *indented* below it.

```
1    # Correct Indentation
2    x = 3
3    if x > 5:
4        print("x is greater than 5")
5    else:
6        print("x is not greater than 5")
```

Incorrect Python Example
In our incorrect example, we are following the same format, *except* that the block after the main clause *is not* indented.

```
1    # Incorrect Indentation
2    x = 3
3    if x > 5:
4    print("x is greater than 5")
5    else:
6    print("x is not greater than 5")
7
```

If you tried to run the second example over the objections of your code editor, you'd see an error like this: "IndentationError: expected an indented block after "if" statement on line 3"

Interestingly, if you put your block after the colon and on the same level as the main clause, Python is OK with it. However, this is not best practice since it can lead to hard-to-read code.

```
1    # Also correct Indentation
2    x = 3
3    if x > 5: print("x is greater than 5")
4    else: print("x is not greater than 5")
5
```

Indentation Rules and Best Practices
So, how do we avoid formatting errors (and frustration)? There are several things to keep in mind as you format your code.

Whitespace Matters:
Languages like Java don't care about whitespace. For Python, whitespace is key to proper formatting. Indentation is done using spaces and tabs. To be consistent, it's best to use tabs and to have the tabs in your code editor set to four spaces. This is common practice in the Python development community. You *could* mix spaces and tabs but that can lead to sloppy and inconsistent formatting and hard-to-read code.

Indentation Levels are Important:
Be consistent when indenting blocks of code. Code block indentation is the hallmark of good Python code and is why it is so easily readable. Four spaces are used for each level of indentation.

Blocks of Code are Defined by Indentation:
In Python, code blocks such as conditionals, loops, and function definitions are defined by indentation. Because of this rule, there is no need to use things like braces to identify and define a block of code. The blocks are obvious just by looking at the shape of the code. Java coders might be thinking: "We use indentation." Yes, we do, but that is mostly out of common practice. In Python, indentation is strictly enforced. If Python's indentation rules are ignored, it will cause an error at run time.

Style is Flexible But There is a Standard:
PEP 8 is Python's style guide and the definitive resource when it comes to best practice. The recommendation for things like four spaces for indentation comes from this guide. If you're using an IDE, and it is set up to use Python rules, it will help you keep your code properly formatted. Most IDEs will flag your code when you have a syntax or formatting error so that you can correct it before run time. By default, most already have tabs set to four spaces.

The Colon Symbol Signals the Start of a Code Block
As touched upon earlier, the start of an indented block of code is signaled by a colon. You'll see them at the end of statements like "if," "else," "for," and "while." You'll also see them used in function definitions. Below is an example of a function definition.

```
1      # Function Definition
2      def greet(name):
3          if name:
4              print("Hello, " + name)
5          else:
6              print("Hello, World")
```

Line 2 gives the name of the function and shows that it can accept a parameter. The colon indicates a block of code is to follow.

Line 3 is an "if" statement and is indented underneath the opening line to indicate that it is part of the function definition as per Python rules. It also ends with a colon to show another statement of code is coming.

Line 4 is indented below line 3 making it clear to Python that this line of code belongs to the "if" statement. There is no colon at the end of this line and there are no other lines after it at the same indentation level. So, Python considers this part of the "if" statement complete.

Line 5 is an "else" statement. It is indented at the same level as the "if" statement because it is part of the function definition. Line 5 ends with a colon indicating that another block of code is to follow. Line 6 is indented underneath the "else" statement signifying it is part of the "else" block. Nothing follows it, so Python considers this block and the function definition to be complete.

If you were to put this into your IDE without the indentations, your IDE would flag it for formatting errors and if you tried to run it anyway, you would get run time errors.

If you think of all this in terms of "block rankings," the outer block encompasses everything indented beneath it. If it has "if/else" statements inside it, they would be indented. Anything inside the "if/else" lines would be indented underneath them. If you had nested "if" statements, the inner "ifs" would be indented inside their outer "ifs." (The more you code in Python, the more this will make sense.)

Code Comments and Best Coding Practices

As simple as Python is to read and understand, I cannot emphasize enough how important and useful code comments can be. Not only are they helpful to other developers who might be collaborating on your code with you, they are helpful to *you* as well. When you're "in the zone" on a coding project, everything is still fresh in your mind, and it all makes sense. Fast forward a few weeks or months later. Someone says they found a use case that is throwing an error, or management says they want you to add a new feature to the code you helped write. Even if you wrote it yourself, when you go back to your old code, you're likely going to have those "what was I thinking" moments. Comments can help make it clear to you and everyone else "what you were thinking."

In Python, comments are preceded by the # (hash, or pound) symbol. Comments can appear above a section of code, or they can appear as an inline comment.

```
1    # This is a comment before a section of code
2    def greet(name):
3        if name:
4            print("Hello, " + name) #This is an inline comment
5        else:
6            print("Hello, World")
7
```

Good practice would be to have the first line give the title for the code and perhaps an additional line or two stating its purpose. For each method or function in the code, you should also include a comment describing what the function/method does. Example:

#Personnel data method

Just by looking at that, I know that this method handles personnel data somehow. I don't have to dig through the code to figure that out, and that comment gives me some context so that I can interpret the code correctly.

In methods and functions that are complex, it's also good to insert comments explaining what the different sections do.

Best Coding Practices
Use descriptive variable names.
Avoid oversimplified names like "count". Is that a total count? A running count? A count of items? A count of iterations? Variable names like "running_count", "total_count", or "item_count" are more descriptive.

If your variable name consists of more than one word, separate each word with an _ (underscore). Example: this_is_a_multiword_variable. Also, when creating variable names, use all lowercase, not mixed case, or camel case.

If you're ever stumped on what best practice is in a given scenario, refer to PEP or just Google it to find out.

Multi-line Comments

To make multi-line comments in Python, precede and follow your multi-line comment with triple quotes. (""" or """). You can use this same syntax to create a multiline string variable. Here is a multi-line example:

```
1    """
2    Lorem ipsum dolor sit amet, consectetur adipiscing elit,
3    sed do eiusmod tempor incididunt ut labore et dolore magna
4    aliqua. Viverra adipiscing at in tellus integer feugiat
5    scelerisque. Amet nisl purus in mollis nunc sed. Massa placerat duis
6    """
7
8    long_quote = """
9    Lorem ipsum dolor sit amet, consectetur adipiscing elit,
10   sed do eiusmod tempor incididunt ut labore et dolore magna
11   aliqua. Viverra adipiscing at in tellus integer feugiat
12   scelerisque. Amet nisl purus in mollis nunc sed. Massa placerat duis
13   """
```

The first one is a comment, the other is populating a variable.

Comment Keyboard Shortcut

Most IDEs support this. If you want to comment out a line quickly, just press CTRL + / and the line the cursor is on will be commented out. You can undo this on a commented line using the same shortcut.

If you want to comment/uncomment multiple lines at once, just highlight the lines you want to do this to and press CTRL + / and all the lines (including any blank lines) will be commented out. This shortcut comes in handy when you want to quickly comment out lines of code to try different coding scenarios.

Case Study: Analyzing a Real-World Python Script

The best way to learn good code is to study good code and see what makes it tick. As we do this case study, we're not going to focus on how each piece *works*. For now, we're just focused on what good code *looks like.*

Key Takeaways

Script Overview: What is the script we're looking at all about? What's its purpose and function?

Code Structure: We'll look at how the code is constructed and how Python indentation rules were applied to make the code clean and readable.

Commenting and Documentation: How did the developer comment their code? Is it clear? Does it spell out for other developers (and the developer's future self), what the code is all about and what each part does?

Best Coding Practices: As we look at this code, we'll see how the developer applied best practices and recommended guidelines.

Highlights: We'll look at select portions of the code and identify key Python syntax features and coding practices.

How We're Going to Dissect This Code

Because this case study includes many lines of code, we're going to break it up into sections and discuss them one section at a time.

Section One:

```
1    # Case Study: Analyzing a Real-World Python Script
2
3    # Script Overview:
4    # This Python script calculates and prints statistics related to a list
5    # of student grades. It computes the average, minimum, and maximum grades,
6    # and identifies students who
7    # scored above the average.
8
9    # Sample student grades:
10   grades = [85, 92, 78, 90, 88, 76, 82, 95, 89, 91]
```

Lines 3-7 give us a clear description of what this script is all about.

Line 9 tells us what the list in line 10 is for.

Section Two:

```
15   # Function to calculate the average grade:
16   def calculate_average(grades):
17       total = sum(grades)
18       return total / len(grades)
19
20   # Function to find the minimum and maximum grades:
21   def find_min_max(grades):
22       return min(grades), max(grades)
23
24   # Function to identify students above the average:
25   def above_average_students(grades, average):
26       above_average = [grade for grade in grades if grade > average]
27       return above_average
```

Good code breaks things into modules where each module has a specific task. We see that here. Each function has one task and the comments

43

above each clearly describe what each function does. Also, note that the code in each function is indented according to PEP 8 guidelines. For example, line 16 is the opening of the "calculate_average" function so it is furthest left. It ends in a colon, so Python "knows" there is more to follow. Lines 17 and 18 are part of that function so they are indented relative to line 16. Because they are both subordinate to line 16, but not to each other, they share the same indent level. Python "knows" line 18 is the end of the function because there is no colon at the end of the line signaling another code block and there is nothing else indented under line 16.

Section Three:

```
29    # Main program:
30    if __name__ == "__main__":
31        # Calculate the average grade
32        average = calculate_average(grades)
33
34        # Find the minimum and maximum grades
35        min_grade, max_grade = find_min_max(grades)
36
37        # Identify students who scored above the average
38        above_avg_students = above_average_students(grades, average)
39
40        # Display the results
41        print("Student Grades:", grades)
42        print("Average Grade:", average)
43        print("Minimum Grade:", min_grade)
44        print("Maximum Grade:", max_grade)
45        print("Students Above Average:", above_avg_students)
```

Lines 31, 34, 37, and 40 all explain what each section of the "main program" does. As in the earlier section, the code is also indented according to PEP 8 guidelines. **Lines 32, 35, and 38** each call the functions defined earlier to populate their respective variables. For example, the variable "average" is populated by a call to "calculate_average()" and includes the "grades" list as a parameter.

Summary:

In our code sample, Python's function structure was used to encapsulate each step of the code's process by using a single function to perform a specific task. Though it might seem to make more sense to put everything into one function, that practice is counterproductive. A singular task per function makes your code easier to debug if issues arise. If everything is in one function, it can be hard to pinpoint the piece of the function causing the issue, and repairing one part of a function could lead to problems in other parts.

Indentation rules were followed throughout the code. If you were to put this into your IDE, you would see no syntax errors and the code would not throw errors at run time.

Finally, the comments throughout the code made it clear what the overall code did and what each section of the code did. This all made for clean and easily readable code.

Project: The GUI Weather App

In this project we'll work on a GUI-based weather app. It will be a program with a simple interface. If you follow along with these projects, not only will you have a better practical understanding of Python, but you'll also have applications that you built to show for it.

In chapters where we do project work, you'll see a "Project" section like this one that will guide you through each step.

IMPORTANT: Please do these steps in your IDE so you can learn how it reacts with your code. Because we are taking a section-by-section approach to writing our app, your IDE may flag certain things as syntax errors. This is normal. Those will clear up as we go.

GUI Weather App Materials
For this project, we'll need two things:

- The Python "requests" library, and

- An API from a weather data provider

Getting the Requests Library
Open a command/terminal prompt. For Windows users, click the Start button, and type "cmd" (without the quotes) in the search input. Then select the "Run as administrator" option. If you're using an IDE like VSCode, you can open a terminal window (CTRL + SHIFT + `). At the prompt, run this command:

```
pip install requests
```

Getting an API
"API" stands for " Application Programming Interface." It is a set of rules for a given application that allows your code to interact with it. APIs are common for most applications.

To get an API for your weather app, go to the "OpenWeather" website and request a free one from there:

https://openweathermap.org/home/sign_up

Be sure to sign up for a *free* account, not a paid one. If you want to get a paid account later, that's up to you, but for this project, we only need the free account. **Once you get your API code, hang onto it! You'll need it later.**

Step One: Creating your File
In your IDE, create a new file called *weather_app.py*.

Step Two: Imports and App Window Setup
Next, you need to import a couple of modules. In your file, write the following lines of code:

```
1   # Create a basic Tkinter window
2   import tkinter as tk
3   import requests
4
5   # Create a window instance
6   window = tk.Tk()
7
8   # Set the window title
9   window.title("Weather Forecast App")
```

Lines 1-3: Line one is a comment. These are used to provide notation in your code and do not affect how your code runs. Lines 2-3 are importing code modules that our code will need. Importing is a common practice in programming. It keeps you from having to reinvent the wheel by using code that already performs tasks that you need.

Line 6: To declare our "window" variable, we are using the statement "tk.TK()". This is creating something called an "instance." In this case, we are creating an instance of the "TK" class which represents the main window for our application. We'll get more into this when we cover Object-Oriented Programming, but the "Tk" class is the blueprint for an application's main window. The "window" variable is an instance of that class, meaning we used the blueprint to build an application window.

Step Three: Adding Window Content

```
11 | # Add content to the window
12   label = tk.Label(window, text="Welcome
     to the Weather Forecast App")
13   label.pack()
```

Please note that **Line 12** is wrapped to fit the page. In your code, line 12 should be one line.

Line 12: Note that on this line we have "tk.Label()". This is a constructor. This one creates an instance of a label widget. "Widget" is a term for a graphical element that you can put on a GUI (graphic user interface) screen.

The "Label" constructor takes a couple of parameters. One is the "window" variable we created earlier. This is so the label "knows" where it lives. The other parameter is a text parameter, so it "knows" what to say.

48

Line 13 uses another Tkinter GUI feature. The ".pack()" method "packs" the label onto our main window. If you want some extra space on either side of the application title when the GUI runs, you can change the ".pack()" part to .pack(padx=10).

I know we have introduced a few concepts that are still new to you. It's hard to teach programming without there being some overlap. Just hang on! The more you see these things, the more they'll start making sense. See you in Chapter 2!

Chapter One Recap!

In this chapter, you've gained some foundational knowledge of Python. You even already have some Python coding experience. Awesome! Don't worry if it all seems crystal clear like mud right now. That's perfectly normal. Work at your own pace, review if you need to and then move on! In Chapter 2, We'll dive deeper into operators and conditional statements, and We'll introduce you to loops. Your journey to becoming a confident Python programmer is just beginning! See you in the next chapter! (You got this!)

W hy is it called "Python"? Python was created by Guido van Rossum. To name his new programming language, he wanted something short, unique, and a little mysterious. At the time, he"'d been reading the published scripts from *Monty Python's Flying Circus*, a popular BBC comedy show from the 1970s. (We allegedly got the term 'spam" from a skit on that show.) He liked the show so much that he decided to name his new programming language in tribute to it. (General Python FAQ, n.d.) It just goes to show that programmers do have a sense of humor. It's warped and quirky, and sometimes lives beyond the grasp of mere mortals, but it does exist.

Section 1: Operators and Expressions

Understanding Operators and Their Role in Python

What are Operators and Why Are They Important?

Operators are essential for any programming language, Python included. They are special symbols used to perform various operations on data. These include mathematical equations, making comparisons, performing logical evaluations, and assigning values. Seeing what they do makes clear why they are so important. They are important because they manipulate data, control program flow, help your code make decisions, give variables their values, and store and retrieve data. Failing to understand how to use operators effectively would be like trying to learn a foreign language without learning any of the verbs. You'd have a hard time communicating anything effectively.

Operator Categories
Operators fall into several broad categories:

Arithmetic Operators: As the name suggests, these are used to perform mathematical calculations. You've seen some of these in action already in chapter one. They include addition (+), subtraction (-), multiplication (*), division (/), integer division (//), modulus a.k.a. remainder (%), and exponentiation (**).

In this example, the code is using subtraction to get a user's birth year:

```
1    #Fun with Operators
2    import datetime #imports datetime module.
3
4    #Asks user to input their birth year
5    birth_year = int(input('What year were you born? '))
6
7    #Get the year from today's date.
8    today = datetime.date.today()
9    current_year = today.year
10
11   #Subtract user's birth year from current year
12   age = current_year - birth_year
13
14   #Print the result
15   print('Your age is ' + str(age))
```

Comparison Operators. These operators compare values and determine the relationship between them. Operators in this category include equal to (==), not equal to (!=), greater than (>), lesser than (<), greater than or equal to (>=), and lesser than or equal to (<=)

In this example, the code checks to see if a student has a passing grade:

```
1   #Fun with Operators
2   student_score = int(input('What is your score? '))
3   passing_grade = 70
4   is_passing = student_score >= passing_grade
5
6   print('Passing = ' + str(is_passing))
```

Line 2 asks the user to enter their score.

Line 3 sets the passing grade at 70.

In **line 4**, "is_passing" is seen by Python as a Boolean (true or false) because comparison operators return "true" or "false" depending on the outcome. In this case, if the student's grade is greater than or equal to the passing grade, the result is "true."

Line 6 shows the user the result.

Logical Operators. These compare multiple conditions and determine whether the overall value of an expression is true. Logical operators include "and," "or," and "not."

This next example uses the logical operator "and" to see if it is a picnic day:

```
1    #Fun with Operators
2    #All three variables are Booleans
3    is_sunny = True
4    is_warm = True
5    is_picnic_day = is_sunny and is_warm
6    print('Is it a picnic day? ' + str(is_picnic_day))
```

Line 5 is a Boolean because logical operators will return true or false based on their evaluation. What is being asked is, "Is it sunny and is it warm?" If the answer to both is true, then the statement returns "true."

Assignment Operators. Assignment operators assign values to variables. The most common assignment variable is the equal sign (=).

Example: x = 7.

When you write code like that in Python, it will determine the variable's type based on the value you assign it. So, for x = 7, Python will determine that x is an INTEGER with the value of 7. If you write x = 7.0, then Python would determine that x is a FLOAT with the value of 7.0.

As simple as the equal sign is, it can be confusing to new programmers because they can mistakenly try to use it as a *comparison* operator. But that operator is ==. What's the difference? The easiest way to keep these straight is to read = and "is" and == as 'same as."

Let's say you had two variables, one named "glass_of_water" and the other named "glass_of_wine" and you wanted to *compare* the two to see if they were the same. If you wrote this in your code: "glass_of_water = glass_of_wine," you'd be asking Python to turn water into wine. Python's powerful, but it's not *that* powerful. Why doesn't that work? Because you're trying to tell Python that "glass_of_water" *is* "glass_of_wine" rather than asking it if the glass_of_water is *the same as* the glass_of_wine. The correct notation would be: "glass_of_water" == "glass_of_wine."

Membership Operators. These operators check to see if a value is a member of a sequence like a list, a string, or a tuple. Membership operators include "in" and "not in."

This example checks if a value is part of a list of fruits:

```
1    #Fun with Operators
2    fruit_list = ["apple", "banana", "cherry","tomato","orange"]
3    test_item = input('What item would you like approved? ')
4    is_approved = test_item in fruit_list
5
6    print('Is ' + test_item + ' approved? ' + str(is_approved))
7
```

The variable "is_approved" is seen by Python as a Boolean because membership operators return a Boolean result. If the user enters "cabbage" as an item, "is_approved" will return "false." If the user enters something that is a member of the list, "is_approved" will return "true."

Creating Expressions and Performing Operations.

Expressions are the heart of computation. But what are we talking about when we talk about "expressions?" We're talking about combining values, variables, and operators in a way that produces accurate and reliable results. Expressions allow you as a programmer to perform something as ordinary as a simple math calculation to a complex logical evaluation designed to analyze scientific data for NASA. The key to becoming proficient with expressions is practice. Don't be afraid to experiment – with your own code – not code from NASA! The more you work with expressions the better you'll understand them. The more you understand them, the more you'll find ways to put them to proper use. Besides just doing simple math, you'll see that expressions can also be used to make decisions and respond to different conditions and inputs.

Example 1 – A Simple Arithmetic Expression
In your IDE create a new file and enter this code:

```
# A simple math expression

total_cost = item_price * quantity
```

Name this file math_expression.py and save it. Your IDE should already be flagging errors. Before you read on, can you tell why?

You've assigned a value to "total_cost" by making it equal to the value of "item_price * quantity." You need to assign values to those two variables. Since the price of things is usually a number with a decimal it should be a float and since the quantity is usually a whole number, that should be an integer. So, change your code to look like this:

```
# A simple math expression

item_price = float(10)

quantity = int(5)

total_cost = item_price * quantity
```

That should have cleared up your syntax errors. What we did is we explicitly declare the numeric data types for item_price and quantity. We could have implicitly declared their types by doing this:

```
item_price = 10.0

quantity = 5
```

From that, Python would have inferred that item_price was a float because the number contained a decimal value, and it would have inferred the quantity was an int because it had a whole number value. At this point, we can run the code in our IDE terminal by making sure we are in the same directory as our code and then running the command:

```
python math_expressions.py
```

The only problem is we won't see anything because we have not told our code how to output it yet. We need to add a print() statement. Remember the print() function has to have a string variable, so We'll need to cast our variable "total_price" as a string. So, add this to the bottom of your code:

```
print("The total cost is " + str(total_cost))
```

Save the code and run it. You should see a result that contains "40.0" We'll worry about properly formatting prices to 2 decimal places later in the book. Just for fun and to help you get more familiar with how expressions behave, take your variable for "item_price" and "quantity" and move them *below* the line that multiplies them. What happens? What happens when you try to run your code like that? Once you've seen go ahead and put your code back to the way it was. When Python reads your expressions, it reads them from the top down. So, if you try to run an operation before you've declared your variables, you'll get errors. Your IDE will warn you of the problem even before you run your code.

Getting User Input

You've already seen the input() function in action in other coding examples. Now let's do that here. The math expression code was fun and all, but it's static. Let's say that this is a cash register program we're writing, and the cashier needs to put in the price per item and the quantity to get a total price. How do we get the cashier's input?

Change your "item_price" and "quantity" variables to look like this:

```
item_price = float(input("What is the cost per item? "))
```

```
quantity = int(input("How many of that item do they have? "))
```

Now save and run your code. With just some minor changes in your expressions, you've gone from a static set of instructions to something a little more dynamic and interactive. There are some concerns here, however. The input() function is very accommodating. It takes a string as a prompt to show the user, and then it accepts any input the user may try to enter. For "item_price" the user could have entered "kittens". The input() function would happily accept them but your code would throw an error. So, we still have some bugs to work out and We'll cover that when we cover error handling.

Example 2 – Conditional Expression
Create a new file called "conditionals.py" in your IDE and enter this code in it:

```
# Conditional Expression
```

```
is_adult = age >= 21
```

You can already see that your IDE has a problem with it. The "age" variable has not been declared. Go ahead and create it but make it so it can accept user input. (Try to do this before reading ahead to my solution.)

Next, add a print line that says, "You are old enough" and shows whether that is true or not.

"Age => 18" uses a conditional operator (greater than or equal to), so it returns a Boolean (true or false) result. Because "is_adult" is assigned the result of our conditional statement, Python infers that "is_adult" is a Boolean data type. This is why your print statement shows "True" or "False" depending on the age you entered.

```
1    # Conditional Expression
2    age = int(input('How old are you? '))
3    is_adult = age >= 21
4
5    print ('You are old enough ' + str(is_adult))
```

To give this some context, let's say that this is an enhancement to our cash register program where the buyer must be a certain age before making certain purchases. Our solution will work, but it's a little awkward. "You are old enough true," or "You are old enough false" sounds a little caveman-y. It would be nice if our code gave one response to a user of the right age and another to a user who is too young. Later in the book, We'll explore exactly how to do that.

Example 3 – String Concatenation Expression
Expressions are not just limited to numbers. They can be used with strings as well. In your IDE create a file called "concat.py" and put this code into it:

```
# String concatenation expression

full_name = first_name + " " + last_name
```

Initialize (declare) the "first_name" and "last_name" variables in a way that accepts user input and then add a print line that says: "Hello, [full_name]" where "full_name" is the concatenation of the other two variables. (Notice that with strings, the concatenation operator is the plus sign ("+").

This is my take on it:

```
1    # String concatenation expression
2
3    first_name = input("What's your first name? ")
4    last_name = input('What\'s your last name? ')
5    full_name = first_name + " " + last_name
6
7    print('Hello, ' + full_name + '!')
```

On line 3, the apostrophe on "What's" works just fine because the whole statement is surrounded by double quotes.

On line 4, however, I have surrounded my statement with single quotes. For the apostrophe to work without causing a syntax error, I had to use an "escape" character, the backslash (\), before the apostrophe. "Escaping" a character means you are telling your programming language to take the character after the \ as a string literal, not a part of your command. If I had left the backslash out, Python would have assumed that my input statement was just "What" and then the IDE would have flagged the rest of the statement as a syntax error. If I had run with it anyway, I would have seen this:

```
PS C:\Users\htack\OneDrive\Programming\Python\2-Diving Deeper into Python> python concat.py
  File "C:\Users\htack\OneDrive\Programming\Python\2-Diving Deeper into Python\concat.py", line 4
    last_name = input('What's your last name? ')
                              ^
SyntaxError: unterminated string literal (detected at line 4)
```

That's Python's way of saying: "Hey, you're missing a quote around one of your strings." Actually, I'm not missing a quote, it's just that I'm using an apostrophe and Python *thinks* it's a quote. The escape (\) character tells Python just to show that single quote as is on the screen and *not* interpret it as a single quotation mark.

Section 2: Conditional Statements

Conditional Statements, also known as "branching statements," or ""if statements," are statements that allow your program to make choices (to branch one way or another) based on the outcome of a condition: "If this is true then do this. Else, do that."

Exploring if, elif, and else Statements.

The "if" Statement

This is probably the most common of conditional statements in programming. The generic syntax for an "if" statement is this:

```
If [test condition] then [result/response]
```

Because of its indentation rules, it looks like this in Python:

```
If [test condition]:

    [result/response]
```

Now let's look at our code from earlier:

```
1    # Conditional Expression
2    age = int(input('How old are you? '))
3    is_adult = age >= 21
4
5    print ('You are old enough ' + str(is_adult))
```

We can improve this a little by applying an "if" statement.:

```
1    # Conditional Expression
2    age = int(input('How old are you? '))
3
4    if age >= 21:
5        print ('You are old enough because you are ' + str(age))
```

That's a little better. If someone is at or above the age of 21, they get a response saying they meet the requirement. But what about people under 21? Right now, they are completely ignored. This is where the "else" statement comes in.

The "Else" Statement

You use the "else" statement for situations where none of your conditions apply. In our case, the condition is the person needs to be 21 or older. To handle users who do not meet that condition, we use the "else" statement. The syntax in Python looks like this:

```
if [condition]:

    [response]

else:

    [catchall response]
```

Note that an "else" statement lives at the same indentation level as its corresponding if statement and its response is indented the same as it is for an "if" statement. So, our improved example will look like this:

```
1    # Conditional Expression
2    age = int(input('How old are you? '))
3
4    if age >= 21:
5        print ('You are old enough because you are ' + str(age))
6    else:
7        print('You\'re only ' + str(age) + '! You\'re too young!')
```

This is good, but what if you have multiple possible conditions? That's where Python's "elif" statement comes in.

The "Elif" Statement

The "elif" (short for "else if") statement allows you to handle multiple conditions before it taps out. Here's an example:

```
1    # Elif example
2    temperature = int(input('What\'s the temperature out side? '))
3    if temperature > 70: #Fahrenheit
4        print("It's too hot outside.")
5    elif temperature > 50:
6        print("It's nice outside.")
7    else:
8        print("It's too cold outside.")
```

Just as with "else" statements, "elif" statements live at the same indentation level as their corresponding "if" statements, and their results are tabbed underneath them.

Conditional statements like "if", "else," and "elif" are all part of the programming journey and are crucial to decision-making logic. They are simple statements to master and very powerful.

Logical Operators

So now you know about "if", "else, and "elif" and you know they are simple and powerful conditional statements, but what about more complex conditions? What if you need to check if more than one thing is true, or part of your condition is seeing whether something is *not* true? This is where logical operators come in.

What are They and How Do They Work?

Logical operators include "and," "or", and "not" and are used to combine or modify conditional statements.

The "and" operator returns true if both conditions are "True". The syntax looks like this:

```
if condition1 and condition2:

    [code if both conditions True]
```

The "or" operator returns true if at least one of the conditions is true. The syntax looks like this:

```
if condition1 or condition2:

    [Code if at least one condition True]
```

When using the "or" operator, put the condition most likely to be true as the first condition (if possible). This is because the code will stop evaluating the conditions as soon as it finds one that is true, and this can help improve performance.

The "not" operator returns the opposite condition. The syntax looks like this:

```
if condition1 or condition2:

    [Code if condition False]
```

To better understand the "not" operator, here's an example:

```
1    # Not operator example for people with monokerophobia:
2    is_unicorns = True
3
4    # Check if there's unicorns
5    if not is_unicorns:
6        print("It's okay. There are no unicorns out there.")
7    else:
8        print("Unicorns! Go to your safe room and lock the doors!")
```

For the record, "monokerophobia" is not a fear of people with nicknames. (That would probably be monikerophobia.) "Monokerophobia" is a fear of unicorns. I found it on the Internet, so it must be true. (Wiki, n.d.)

Coding Challenge: Walk the Dog

Nested "if" statements are a common occurrence in programming. For this challenge I want you to use a nested "if" statement. So, remember your indentation rules. The coding solution you're going to make checks to see if it's OK to walk the dog. Here are the parameters:

- Create a file called "walk_the_dog.py". You can walk the dog if it's sunny or cloudy.

- In your code, have a line that asks the user what the weather is like.

- Include this list of weather conditions: ['sunny","cloudy","rainy"]

- Have your outer "if" check to see if what the user has entered exists in the list. The syntax looks like this:

  - [item_name] in [list_name]. This will return a Boolean result.

  - If the weather condition the user entered is not in the list, have your code print: "We ain't going nowhere! That's unicorn weather!"

- Have your inner "if" use "if", "elif", and "else" statements and at least one logical operator. Hint: Two of your weather conditions are suitable for dog walking. So, you might want to test for those together.

o Based on the weather condition, have your code print whether it is OK or not OK to walk the dog and why: "It's OK/not OK to walk the dog because it's [weather_condition] outside.

The answer to this one is in the back of the book. Try this on your own before you look at my answer.

Section 3: Loops and Iteration

Iterating through data is another common programming task. This is done using loops. Like conditional statements, loops are simple but powerful tools, and when used properly can save time especially when there are many lines of data involved.

Introduction to For and While Loops

The For Loop

In Python, the "for loop" is an iterating function, meaning it is something that repeatedly executes a set of instructions over several, sometimes many, items a specified number of times. "For" loops in Python are used to iterate over objects like lists, tuples, dictionaries, and even strings – things that typically have a sequence and a defined start and finish.

The syntax of a "for" loop looks like this:

```
for iterator_variable in sequence_object:
        Code…
```

The words "for" and "in" are italicized to emphasize that these are keywords that must be part of the "for" loop statement. To better understand this, let's look at a code example:

```
1    # Iterating through a list
2    shopping_list = ['milk','eggs','bacon','coldcuts','bananas']
3
4    for item in shopping_list:
5        print (item)
```

In this sample, "shopping_list" is a list object. Lists are surrounded by square brackets with the items inside them separated by commas. The variable "item" is populated in the "for" statement. Python knows that "item" refers to anything in the list. Indented underneath the "for" statement is the command to print each item in the list. If you run this code, you'll see the list of items printed vertically. This simple example only prints the items, but any number of actions could have been taken on the items in the list. The loop knows to start at the beginning of the list and continue to the end unless a condition inside the loop instructs it to stop.

The While Loop

Like the "for" loop, the "while" loop is an iterative function. Unlike the "for" loop, however, a "while" loop will continue as long as the condition it is told to check remains true. The syntax for a "while" loop looks like this:

```
while condition:

     code...
```

To better understand this, let's look at an example:

```
1    # While loop example
2    count = 0
3    while count < 10:
4        print(count)
5        count += 1
```

First, **Line 2** sets a counter. "While" loops do not always have to be set using counters, but they often are. **Line 3** of the code sets the condition the while loop needs to check. As long as the counter is less than 10, the loop will continue. **Line 4** prints the count. **Line 5** introduces us to a new operator, the plus-equals operator (+=). It is a shorthand way of saying, "count = count + 1." There are other similar operators: minus-equals(-=), times-equals (*=) and divide-equals (/=).

The increment operator has an opposite called the decrement operator and looks like this: -=. As you might have guessed the decrement subtracts the given amount from the variable it is given.

If you run this code, you'll see the numbers 0-9 printed vertically in the terminal. This is because when the counter reaches the number 10, the loop stops. If you want the numbers up to 10, you would have to change **Line 3** to read: while count <= 10.

Infinite Loops
"While" loops can be set to run "forever" if you fail to put in a proper check. For example, if you left out **Line 5**, the loop would not stop, and you would see a continuous series of zeroes on the screen because the counter would not increment and the count would never equal 10. "Forever" is in quotes because you would either run out of memory, or

the IDE would force the code to stop if you could not – but not until you caused a serious rift in the fabric of time and space. (Just kidding, sort of.)

Iterating Dictionaries and Other Data Types

We looked at iterating a list, but I also mentioned that loops could iterate other data types. Anything that holds data in some sort of sequence can be iterated by a loop. This would even include large tables of data from things like spreadsheets and databases. We'll cover that in more detail when we get to data analysis. For now, here is a code example showing how to use a "for" loop to iterate a dictionary:

```
1    # Looping through a dictionary
2    person = {"name": "Alice", "age": 30, "city": "Wonderland"}
3    for key, value in person.items():
4        print(f"{key}: {value}")
5
```

A dictionary is a set of data with key-value pairs where each value in the dictionary is tied to a unique key. **Line 5** introduces something new: the "f-string." This tells Python to format the output according to the format shown in the string after the "f." In this case, it will show the data in the format of "key: name."

Coding Challenge: Shopping Help

When my wife sends me to the grocery store with a shopping list, I sometimes have to call her to figure out where stuff is: "Hey, if I were cottage cheese, where would I be?" And she would say: "Oh, that's in _____," or "That's in _____." For this challenge, I want you to write code using a "for" loop, "if", "elif" and "else" statements. Here are the parameters:

Create a file in your IDE and call it `shopping_help.py.`" Use these lists in your code:

```
shopping_list =
["milk","eggs","bacon","coldcuts","bananas"]

dairy = ["milk","yogurt","cheese","ice cream","butter"]

meat = ["beef","pork","bacon","coldcuts"]

fruit = ["apples", "bananas", "oranges"]
```

Iterate the shopping list with a "for" loop.

Use the other lists to print what the item is and what section it would be in. Example: "bacon is in meats."

If an item is not in any list, print: "Can't find [item]? Ask somebody!"

To see if something is in a list, the syntax is:

`[item_name] in [list_name].` This returns a Boolean result.

To save yourself some frustration, enter your inputs in lowercase. There is one item in the shopping list that does not have a category. All the others do. The answer is in the back of the book. Try first, then look.

Project: The GUI Weather App

In this section we're defining functions for our weather app. The functions in our app will do the heavy lifting in our code. Don't worry if you don't understand what you're coding just yet. We'll be explaining functions in the next chapter.

Step Four: Defining the "fetch_weather" Function

Add these lines to your code.

```
15   # Function to fetch weather based on
     user input
16  def fetch_weather():
17      location = location_entry.get()
18      weather_data = get_weather(location)
19      display_weather(weather_data)
```

Remember, the lines are wrapped to fit the page.

Line 16 demonstrates the syntax used to define a function: It is the name of the function followed by a pair of parentheses and a colon. Note how everything that is part of the function is indented in from the "def" line.

Line 17 will capture the user's entry from the input field (not created yet) to populate the "location" variable.

Line 18 will populate the "weather_data" variable by making a call to the "get_weather" function (not written yet) by passing it the value of "location."

Line 19 will call the "display_weather" function (not written yet) and pass the value of "weather_data" into it.

So, now you've been introduced to functions. In Chapter 3 we'll learn more about them!

Chapter Two Recap!

In this chapter, we took a deep dive into several key programming building blocks to expand your Python programming skills and you also had some programming challenges where you were able to apply those skills for yourself. Here's a brief recap of what we explored:

- **Operators and Expressions:** We talked about how expressions are used to perform various operations on data, including arithmetic, logical operators, and comparisons. We also looked at the difference between the assignment operator (=) and the comparison operator (==). Expressions are essential to manipulating and analyzing data and can be used to solve real-world problems.

- **Conditional Statements:** We looked at conditional statements using "if," "elif," and "else." We learned that these statements can help our code make decisions based on the outcomes of those conditions. As part of our discussion, we also looked at logical operators ("and", "or", and "not") and how they can help construct more complex conditions. And with the "Walk the Dog" challenge you had an opportunity to apply that for yourself.

- **Loops and Iteration:** We also learned about the power of "for" and "while" loops and discussed the difference between the two. Loops help us to perform repetitive tasks efficiently and can help us iterate through objects like lists, dictionaries, tuples, and more. The "Shopping Help" challenge allowed you to use loops to go through a list and use the list to refer to other lists and categorize things.

In Chapter 3, "Building Python Functions," We'll look at functions, another fundamental aspect of Python programming. Functions provide modularity so that you can dedicate portions of your code to specific tasks, making for more efficient code, easier debugging, and faster and more efficient development. Here's a preview of what We'll cover:

- **Defining Functions.** We'll look at what functions are, what they are used for, and how to define them in Python. You'll learn how to create your own custom functions so that you can learn how to encapsulate blocks of code and make them reusable.

- **Parameters and Arguments.** Parameters and arguments are a way to allow your functions to communicate with each other. With them, you can pass data to other functions and customize their behavior, making for flexible and adaptable code.

- **Return Statements.** Master the art of return statements, which allow your functions to produce results and share data with the rest of your code. Return statements are the other side of the function "conversation." Where parameters and arguments send data into a function, return statements send data out. You'll learn how to create return statements and how to utilize their output.

3 BUILDING PYTHON FUNCTIONS

L et's say you're at a gathering of friends. You're talking, eating, having a good time, and then the host of this get-together comes out with a cardboard box and announces: "Hey, I've got this puzzle." He's got the box held high so no one can see inside it yet. He shakes it and says, "I've had this thing a while, but I never put it together because I lost the cover with the picture. I think it's supposed to be an old barn in the Fall surrounded by trees. You wanna give it a shot?"

There's some hesitation at first, but then someone says, "Sure, why not?" So, your friend dumps the contents of the box onto a table, and you all gather around.

When dealing with code, you might get handed a coding puzzle. The problem might be clearly defined, but it might not be.

When you're working on a puzzle, you might have the cover to the box, you might not. In either case, the first step is often to organize the pieces into logical groupings: "sky" pieces in one group, "ground" pieces in another, maybe corner pieces arranged at each corner, etc. Functions in programming are a little like that process. When you write them, they need to address the problem, but like the "corner" pieces of your puzzle task, functions are designed to handle a specific piece of the problem.

In this chapter on "Building Python Functions," We'll learn how to define a function, how to build it, and how to apply it to a specific task.

Section 1: Defining Functions

What are Functions?

"A Python function is a block of organized, reusable code that is used to perform a single, related action. Functions provide better modularity for your application and a high degree of code reusing." (Python - Functions, n.d.)

Of the definitions I reviewed for this section, I liked this one because it covered the main characteristics of what makes for a good Python function:

- **Organization:** Functions are designed to keep your code organized, logical, and clear.

- **Singularity:** Each function you write should define a clear and single action.

- **Modularity:** While this sounds a lot like singularity, this feature of functions speaks to coding philosophy. When you code, you need to think in terms of coding in modules that come together to form the whole. It's a little like working with Lego® blocks.

- **Reusability:** This builds on the modularity idea. Functions are meant to be reusable. Just like you can use a Lego® brick to build a firetruck, you can also use it to build a house.

Okay, now that we've defined what a function is, let's define one of our own.

Function Syntax

Basic function syntax should look like this:

```
1    # Basic function syntax
2    def function_name(parameters):
3        # Function body
4        # As with all things Python, indentation matters.
5        # All code in a function must be indented.
6        # Functions can have multiple statements.
```

The Parts of a Function

- "def": This is the keyword that declares a Python function.

- Function name: Function names in Python are not limited to any particular part of speech. They can be anything, but they do follow certain rules:

    o   They must be lowercase.

    o   Words in multiword function names must be separated by underscores. This is called "snake case." (The programming language is called "Python," after all.) Example: this_is_a_multiword_function_name

- Parentheses: Function names must end with a set of parentheses, even if they do not take any parameters.

- Function Body: As already mentioned in the coding example, all the statements in a function must be indented beneath the function name.

Parameters

Unlike strongly typed languages like Java where you must declare a type on parameters, in Python you *do not*. This falls in line with Python's philosophy of code clarity and readability. It can get away with this because it uses something called "dynamic typing," meaning Python determines a parameter's type at runtime. As you have already seen, it does the same with variables. You can, however, use "type hints," where you can give hints as to what the parameter types are. Here is an example of a function with type hints:

```
1    # Type hint example
2    def count_blessings(blessing_num: int, blessing_name: str):
3        # Function with multiple parameters
4        # Parameters have type optional hints
```

Type hints are not a Python requirement and Python will not enforce any kind of typing rules at runtime. However, hints are helpful to you and other developers if the type is not obvious, or if you have multiple parameters of different types.

Calling Functions

Another way to describe a function is to say that it is a block of code that runs when it's called. That's probably why Python is called "Python" and not "Feline" because then functions would never run when called. (Pause for laughter.)

So, how do you call a function? Below is an example of a function call:

```
1    # Function call example.
2    # Here is the function:
3    def greet(name):
4        print(f"Hello, {name}!")
5
6    # Here is the function call:
7    greet("Alice")
```

In this example, the function accepts a "name" parameter and then prints a greeting. To format the greeting correctly, the print function has an "f string" in it. The "f" = "formatted." It tells Python that the string it's about to print must be formatted in a certain way. What you see in the print statement is: (f"Hello, {name}!") The curly braces around "name" let Python know that this is a parameter, meaning it should print the contents of the parameter that was passed in. This way, it prints "Hello, Alice!" and not "Hello, {name}!"

In the function call, you see that it is just the name of the function with the parameter in parentheses. A function call can be a standalone statement as you see in our example, or it can be called from inside another function or method.

Let's Write a Function

Remember our puzzle analogy? Let's solve one. Open your IDE and create a file called "function_example.py." Then follow the steps below to solve our coding puzzle.

Step 1 - The puzzle

We need to create a function that determines the area of a rectangle, and then we need to call it. Remember: to get the area of a rectangle, you need to multiply the width by the length.

Step 2 – Define the Function

The first thing we need to do is come up with a name for our function. It needs to be simple and clear. So, let's go with "area_calculator." You could also use something with "rectangle" in the name if you want. The point is that you want function names that easily identify what the function does. The definition line should look like this:

```
1    # Definition
2    def area_calculator(width, length):
```

Step 3 – Function Body

The body of your function needs to be indented below the definition. So, it should look like this:

```
1    # Definition
2    def area_calculator(width, length):
3        area = length * width
4        return area
5
```

In this example, we declare the variable "area" and assign it the result of width * length. Then we return "area." You could shorten this by leaving out the variable and just returning the result of the formula like this:

```
1    # Definition
2    def area_calculator(width, length):
3        return length * width
4
```

Step 4 – Calling the Function

Now let's call the function from the print() function.

```
1    # Definition
2    def area_calculator(width, length):
3        return length * width
4
5    # Calculate the area
6    area = area_calculator(5, 3)
7    print(f"The area of the rectangle is {area} square units.")
```

Step 5 – Check Your Work

In the terminal window of your IDE, run the program by running this:

```
python area_calculator
```

You should get back the result of 15. Test it with other numbers as well, including decimal numbers to make sure it works as expected.

Section 2: Parameters and Arguments

What Are Parameters and Arguments?

Parameters are the variables that appear between the parentheses in a function definition. In the previous section, our function parameters were "width" and "height." These were the values being passed into our function.

Arguments are values you pass to a function when you call it. Again, going back to our previous example, we called our function with two arguments, a 3 and a 5:

```
area_calculator(3, 5)
```

Go back to your function, remove the arguments from the function call, and see what happens. When you try to call a function that expects parameters, but you don't include the arguments in your function call, you'll get an error. If a function has two parameters, and you send in only one, you will also get an error.

Now go back to your function, enter your numbers with single quotes around each, and see what happens. You sent in two arguments, but you sent them in as the wrong type. You sent them in as strings instead of numbers. When you call a function, you need to respect the number of arguments as well as the type of arguments the function is expecting.

Creating Versatile Functions with Varying Inputs

When writing code, the better you can anticipate how a user might interact with your program, the more you can improve the user experience. Functions in Python are powerful and versatile in this way because they allow you to write code that can respond to different scenarios.

Default Parameters

In the function we wrote for section one when you left out the arguments, you got an error. This is because when a function is designed to expect errors and you provide none, the function will throw an error. With default parameters, you can anticipate scenarios where an argument might be missing. In your function, change the definition to look like this:

```
def area_calculator(width =2, length = 2):
```

Now, call the function with no arguments and see what happens. Try it again with just one parameter. Because you had default values for your parameters, Python had what it needed for that function and was able to return a result.

This behavior isn't just good for handling user errors; it's also good for scenarios where there is an expected default behavior, and a variation is the exception. Let's say the company you work for makes 2x2 squares. Occasionally there are exceptions, but mostly they make 2x2 squares. With the modification to our function definition, we don't have to remember to enter "2, 2" in our area_calculator function. We can just call the function without arguments and get the 2x2 result we expect.

Arbitrary Argument Lists

In our function we knew there would only be two arguments needed because we were calculating area: width * length. But what happens if you know your function needs to work with a list of parameters, but that list can vary? For example, let's say you want to create a grocery list app. How would you make a function flexible enough to accept a list that could change from week to week? This is where "*args*" and "**kwargs" can help you.

*Using *args*

The "*args" argument allows you to accept a non-keyword list of arguments. To use an "*args" parameter in your function you prefix the parameter with an asterisk followed by the parameter name. Let's try it out. Go ahead and create a file in your IDE and call it, "flex_param.py."

We're going to create an "arg" function demo. So, let's define it like this:

```
1    # *arg param demo
2    def arg_func(*items):
```

Now let's show ourselves the kind of data type we're using:

```
1    # *arg param demo
2    def arg_func(*items):
3        print(f"Data type of argument: {type(items)}")
```

In line 3 in the screenshot above, notice how we are getting the data type. Inside the curly braces, we have "type(items)". This comes in handy when you're not entirely clear about what kind of data type is being used in a section of code.

Now, let's add a print statement and follow that up with a function call so we know what's in our items list:

```
1    # *arg param demo
2    def arg_func(*items):
3        print(f"Data type of argument: {type(items)}")
4
5        for item in items:
6            print(item)
7
8    arg_func('bananas', 'strawberries','toothpaste','paper towels')
```

When you run this, notice that it is a "tuple," and ordered list. Because it's a list, we were able to iterate it (lines 5-6) and have it do something with the items in the list. In our case, we just printed them.

Using **kwargs

While it would make for a great Klingon name, the keyword "kwargs" is short for "keyword arguments" and is used for parameters that contain key-value pairs. A key-value pair is a list of items where each item in the list is identified by a unique key.

Let's add another function to our "flex_param.py" code:

```
10    # **kwargs param demo
11    def kwarg_func(**data):
12        print(f"Data type of argument: {type(data)}")
13
14        for key, value in data.items():
15            print(f"{key} is {value}")
```

In line 12 we're showing ourselves the data type we're using, and in lines 14-15 we're iterating the list and formatting the output to show us the key and its corresponding value. The blank space at line 13 is not required, but I do it to break things up within my code blocks for clarity. It's clear that lines 14-15 are a "for" loop and have a purpose distinct from the opening lines of the function.

"Polymorphism"

Polymorphism (a.k.a. function overloading) based on parameter types is not supported by Python as it is in other languages. To give you a rough idea of this kind of polymorphism, let's say we have the language "J." In "J," I can have two methods by the same name like this:

```
brewCoffee(String brand)
```

```
brewCoffee(String brand, int quantity)
```

These both have the same name. How would my code "know" which one I wanted? It would know by the parameters I entered. The first one only takes a single parameter of type String. The other takes two parameters, one of type String and one of type int. If I wrote "brewCoffee("Maxwell House")," it would know I meant the first method. If I wrote "brewCoffee("Maxwell House", 2)," it would know I meant the second one.

Python can mimic this kind of polymorphism by using a non-default parameter followed by default parameters:

```
def add(a, b=0, c=0):
    return a + b + c

print(add(1))
print(add(1, 2))
print(add(1, 2, 3))
```

In the above example, I was able to call the "add" function with three different sets of parameters. This is because parameters "b" and "c" have defaults set on them. This is not true polymorphism. Even though in the first function call I only have 1 parameter, Python still thinks it's getting 3 because the other two have already been set to "0."

If you were to run this code, you would get an error:

```
def add(a, b=0, c=0):
    return a + b + c

def add(a,b):
    return a + b

print(add(1, 2, 3)) # The code would error here.
print(add(1,2)) # The code would not reach here
print(add(1)) # or here.
```

The code would throw an error at the first function call `print(add(1,2,3))` and tell you this:

`TypeError: add() takes 2 positional arguments but 3 were given`

Why would it say that? First, because Python reads the code from the top down. Second, Python cannot accept duplicate function names even if the parameters are different. It will see the first method but when it runs into the second one with the same name, it will see it as a *replacement* of the first. Hence, the error.

This subsection introduced you to the concept of creating versatile Python functions that can adapt to varying inputs. We highlighted the use of default values, and arbitrary argument lists so that you can write code to handle different scenarios. We also briefly discussed polymorphism and how we can get Python to mimic that functionality even though it does not support it. Now let's look at a real-world example so you can see these concepts used in a practical way.

Case Study: A Real-World Function with Practical Use
Our Scenario:
We want to create a library catalog. It will store information about the books in the collection, including title, author, etc. This information will be stored in a list. Users can then search this list based on different criteria. For this example, we'll focus on the sorting functionality.

Optional:
You can simply read along as we walk through this code, or you can create your own Python file and write the code as you read to get more familiar with the syntax and thought process behind coding in Python.

Problem:

Our function needs to be able to accept lists of books and respond to the user's sort criterion. To make this work, we need to have a built-in list of allowable search options and be able to respond to user errors when they choose an option that is not allowed.

Looking Ahead

In this real-world example, we are going to use two concepts we have not covered yet: lambda functions and the "raise Exception" syntax.

Defining the Function

Here is the function we will use for the library catalog:

```
1    # Library Catalog Demo
2    def sort_books(book_list, sort_option):
3        # Check if the criterion is valid
4        valid_criteria = ["title", "author", "publication date"]
5        if sort_option not in valid_criteria:
6            raise ValueError("Invalid sorting criterion")
7
8        # Use the Python `sorted` function with a
9        # lambda function as the key
10       sorted_list = sorted(book_list, key=lambda book:
11                            book[sort_option])
12
13       return sorted_list
```

Let's go through this line by line:

Line 2: This is the function definition. It takes two parameters: a list called "book_list" and a string called "sort_option."

Line 4: This declares the list "valid_criteria."

Line 5: This takes the user's "sort_option" and checks it against the "valid_criteria" list. It uses a "not in" statement to see if the user entered an invalid search option.

Line 6: This line uses the "raise Exception" syntax. In this case, if the user enters an invalid search option, it raises the ValueError exception and shows the user the custom message: "Invalid sorting criterion." For a list of Python's built-in exceptions, you can go to this site:

https://docs.python.org/3/library/exceptions.html

Line 10: If the user's sort option is allowed, then the list is sorted according to the user's choice. To perform this sort, the function uses Python's built-in "sorted" function. To see a complete list of Python's built-in functions and their syntax, you can go to this site:

https://docs.python.org/3/library/functions.html

The "sorted" function has one required and two optional parameters.

- The word "iterable" means it takes an iterable item like a list or a dictionary. This parameter is required.

- The "key" is optional and defaulted to "none." If it is included, it must point to a key in the key-value pair that is being sorted.

- The "reverse" option is defaulted to "False." If set to true, it reverses the sort order.

In our real-world example, the call to the "sorted" function uses the key and populates it with a "lambda." The "lambda" function is also known as an anonymous function. Think of it as a dummy function when a function needs a function as a parameter. The "key" option in the "sorted" function requires a function as a parameter and a "lambda" suits that purpose.

The syntax for a "lambda" looks like this:

```
lambda arguments: expression
```

In our example, the "key" option we are using looks like this:

```
key=lambda book:book[sort_option]
```

To put this into plain English we are telling the key, "Lambda is your function. The argument that function takes is book. The "sort" key you're going to use is whatever sort_option the user happened to pick." So, if the user happens to pick "author" as their sort key, all the books in the book_list will be sorted by author. Don't worry if it feels like your mind went on vacation during that explanation. The more you use the "sorted" function and the more you use "lambdas" the more they will make sense. Knowledge like this takes time to develop.

Line 12: This returns the sorted list once the function completes the sort.

Populating the Library
Now that the function is in place, we need to populate the library. The library is a list of dictionary objects. Dictionaries are lists that have key-value pairs where each value in the dictionary is identified by a key. Here is our library:

```
# Sample list of books
library = [
    {"title": "Python for Beginners", "author": "Glenn Haertlein", "publication date" : "TBD"},
    {"title": "Python for Beginners", "author": "Alice Smith", "publication date": "2022-01-15"},
    {"title": "The Art of Coding", "author": "Bob Johnson", "publication date": "2020-05-10"},
]
```

Calling the Function
Here are some sample function calls. The last one is incorrect:

```
# Sort by title
sorted_by_title = sort_books(library, "title")

# Sort by author
sorted_by_author = sort_books(library, "author")

# Sort by publication date
sorted_by_date = sort_books(library, "publication date")

# Sort by rating (This one is invalid)
sorted_by_rating = sort_books(library, "rating")

print(sorted_by_title)
```

If we run this now, the "print" command will not run because the last function call wants to sort by a sort option that is not allowed. So, the code will raise that error we mentioned earlier:

```
ValueError("Invalid sorting criterion")
```

When that is removed, the "print" request to show the books sorted by title will run:

```
[{'title': 'Python for Beginners', 'author': 'Glenn Haertlein', 'publication
date': 'TBD'}, {'title': 'Python for Beginners', 'author': 'Alice Smith', 'pu
blication date': '2022-01-15'}, {'title': 'The Art of Coding', 'author': 'Bob
Johnson', 'publication date': '2020-05-10'}]
```

In our next section, we'll cover something you have already seen by way of example: return statements. Return statements are how functions can communicate feedback to the code that called it.

Section 3: Return Statements

The Power of Return Statements

Return statements serve as the bridge between a function's internal logic and the rest of your program. Going back to our puzzle analogy, you have that group of the puzzle team who are in charge of the 'sky" pieces. Since the subject of the puzzle was a barn, you also have the group in charge of the "barn pieces," and so on. While each group is working on a particular section of the puzzle, the goal is for each to share the results of their work with the group. You expect that the "sky piece" people are returning an image of the sky and that the "barn" people are building the image of the barn and so on.

Return statements on functions are a little like that. They each have their specific task and when they are done, they should return what they were assigned to do. We have seen that several times already, even with our most recent example.

Leveraging Return Statement Results

Functions do not exist in a vacuum. They are used to complete complex tasks. The power of functions comes from the fact that you can break complex problems into smaller more manageable tasks and leverage what they return to produce the more complex result.

Example: Reading a File

Combing through a file might not be a complex task, but it can be a very monotonous and time-consuming one. If you have hundreds of files to process, each with thousands of lines of data, that task can take a very long time. A function can handle tasks like that quickly and efficiently, even if it has many files and many lines of data. Here is an example:

```
1    import csv
2
3    def csv_file_reader(file_path):
4        file_data = []
5        with open(file_path, 'r') as file:
6            csv_reader = csv.DictReader(file)
7            for row in csv_reader:
8                file_data.append(row)
9        return file_data
```

Line 1: You have seen import statements in some of our other examples. The "import" keyword is used to make the code in one module available to another. For a list of Python's built-in imports, you can visit this site:

https://docs.python.org/3/py-modindex.html

Our example is importing Python's csv module. A "CSV" is a comma-separated values file. This means the data points in each row of data are separated by commas (or some other separator like semicolons (;)). Our reader is designed to "read" this data so that our code can use it.

Line 3: This is our function definition, and it takes a file path. This is so our code can know where to find the file that needs to be processed.

Line 4: This is creating an empty list called "file_data." This will store the lines of data from the file into a list that can be iterated for further analysis.

Line 5: This line introduces us to the "with" keyword. For now, think of it as a means of opening a resource for processing and then closing the resource when it's done. What we are telling our code is: "With this object, do the following tasks." In our "with" statement we are opening the file provided by the user. The "r" in the "open" statement opens the file in read mode as opposed to write mode because we just want to read the contents, not change anything. The "as file" statement is simply assigning a variable name to the object being read.

Line 6: This is assigning a Python CSV reader object to the variable "csv_reader" so that the contents of the CSV can be processed.

Lines 7-8: This for loop iterates through the csv_reader and puts each line of data into the file_data list created earlier.

Line 9: The return statement returns the contents of the file to the rest of the program.

With the data from the return statement, you could create another function called "find_rows" that accepts lists and search strings as parameters. The "find_rows" function could then be tasked to find rows with specific data strings to put into a new, more streamlined file with only the data needed by the user, or some other function in your code.

A Personal Example

At the company where I work, we have files that we process that are too large for the commercial spreadsheet software we normally use. On top of that, the files are so large that most of the laptops used by our company cannot open them, let alone pull the needed data from them. To handle this, I wrote a program that could process the files a line at a time, rather than all at once, pull only the needed lines of data, and then format the data in a way that the commercially available spreadsheet program could consume – and this could all be done using any company laptop. To accomplish all this meant breaking the tasks into smaller, manageable functions that shared their data with each other so that they could accomplish the larger task.

Project: The Gui Weather App

In the previous chapter, you were introduced to functions by building one of the three we need for our app. Now that you have a better understanding of functions, let's add two. Then, in Chapter Four we'll add the finishing touches.

Step Five: Defining the "get_weather" Function

Add these lines of code to create the "get_weather" function. The first line of the definition must be on the same indent level as the precious function.

```
21   def get_weather(location):
22       api_key = 'YOUR_API_KEY'
23       unit='imperial'
24       params = {'q':location, 'appid':
         api_key, 'units':unit}
25       response = requests.get(
         weather_api_url, params=params)
```

Line 21 defines our new function. This one takes an argument called "location".

Line 22 needs the API key you got earlier. Be sure to surround it in quotes.

Line 23 declares the "unit" parameter. Note that it is "unit" *singular*, not plural. In the example, I have it set to 'imperial' to get the temperature in Fahrenheit. You can change that to something else if you prefer.

Line 24 populates the "params" variable. In that variable we are formatting our request in the way "Open Weather" API expects to receive it.

Line 25 populates the response variable. To get its data, it uses the "requests" module we imported earlier to send the request to Open Weathers's API.

The "if" statement
There is an "if" statement below line 25 that needs to start *at the same indent level* as line 25. That's because it is part of the "get_weather" function.

```
27         if response.status_code == 200:
28             data = response.json()
29             return data
30         else:
31             return None
```

Line 27-28 should look a little familiar to you. It's a conditional. If our request comes back with a status code of 200, it means our request to the API was accepted and we have data coming back.

Line 29 is also part of the "if" statement. The "return" keyword will give us the data we received from the API.

Lines 30-31 is what our code's response will be if we get anything other than a status code of 200. Instead of capturing an error message, we're just going to have our code return nothing. This will keep it from crashing, or showing our user an error code. Instead, it will just allow the user to try again. IMPORTANT: Not that in our return statement that "None" is capitalized. That is a Python requirement. It will not recognize "none," or "null."

Step Six: Defining the "display_weather" Function

To get the weather data that you'll display in your GUI app, add these lines of code:

```
33   # Function to display weather data
34   def display_weather(data):
35       result_label.config(text="")
36       if data:
37           temperature = data['main']['temp']
38           description = data['weather'][0][
             'description']
39           message = f'Temperature: {temperature
             } \xb0F\nDescription: {description}'
40           result_label.config(text=message)
41       else:
42           result_label.config(text='Failed to
             fetch weather data.')
```

Line 34 declares the definition of our "display_weather" function and must be at the same indent level as our previous functions.

Line 35 "result_label" is a Tkinter widget that we are leaving blank for now. It will change based on the results we get from the API.

Lines 36-42 is a conditional statement. If we get a correct response from Open Weather's API, it will return JSON data that our code will parse into a human-readable message in our GUI.

Line 29 has some notation in it to render the degree symbol in the temperature and a line break to put the description on a separate line. The notation \xb0 is the Unicode escape sequence for the degree symbol. The notation \n is an escape sequence that tells the code to render the text after it on a new line. The capital F is for the unit of measure chosen in the example (Fahrenheit).

We're almost done! In Chapter 4, we'll add the finishing touches.

Chapter 3 Recap!

In this chapter, you learned how to create versatile, result-driven functions. You've also discovered the power of return statements, and how they help your functions communicate their results. We these tools and this knowledge you are now able to design functions that can make your Python applications efficient and effective.

In Chapter 4 We'll look at fundamental data types in Python such as lists, dictionaries, and sets in greater detail than we have already. We'll see how they can be used to build more robust Python applications and how to use them for data storage and management.

4 DATA STRUCTURES IN PYTHON

Python's data structure capabilities are powerful enough to handle everything from simple to-do lists to complex data management. In this chapter, we'll be diving into Python's data structures.

Section 1: Lists and Tuples

Understanding Lists and Tuples

You have already seen these by this point in the book, but let's take a deeper look.

In Python, lists and tuples are data objects that can store collections of items. Both have something called an "index" that identifies each item in the collection. The index in these objects starts at 0, meaning if you want to get the first item in a list or tuple, you would ask for the item at index 0: `print(my_list[0])`. Both lists and tuples maintain order, can be sorted, and can contain heterogeneous collections, meaning that a single list, for example, can contain strings, integers, and floats at the same time.

Lists are mutable, meaning you can change them at any time. Tuples are not. For example, if you were building a task manager app, you could use a list to store tasks because tasks can change at any time:

```
task = []
```

But let's say you're building a scheduling program, and you need to maintain a collection of weekdays. Since the names for the days of the week don't change, you'd want to use a tuple:

```
weekdays = ('Sunday", "Monday", "Tuesday", "Wednesday",
"Thursday", "Friday", "Saturday")
```

Indexing, Slicing, and Manipulating Data

Indexing

As already mentioned, you can get to any single member of a list or tuple using an index. But there may be times when you want more than one but not all the items from the list or tuple. "slicing" lets you do just that.

Slicing

To slice a list, tuple, or string, you specify the starting index and the ending index. You can also include an optional 'step" that indicates what you want to skip within the slice. The syntax looks like this:

```
sequence[start:end:step]
```

"sequence" is the name of the sequence you want to slice. From our earlier tuple example, we had a sequence called "weekdays."

"start" is the beginning index for the section you want. The start is *inclusive*, meaning it is considered part of the slice.

"end" is the last index of the section you want. The end is *exclusive*, meaning it is *not* included in the slice. The example below will help to illustrate this.

Using our scheduling program scenario, let's say you're using it to keep track of a class schedule. "Underwater Basket Weaving" meets on Monday, Wednesday, and Friday. To get just those days from your "weekdays" variable, your code would look like this:

```
class_days = weekdays[1:6:2]
```

Remember, we declared our weekday sequence like this:

```
weekdays = ("Sunday", "Monday", "Tuesday", "Wednesday",
"Thursday", "Friday", "Saturday")
```

"Sunday" is at index 0 because all indices start with 0. "Saturday" is at index 6. We're making that our endpoint because we want "Friday," so we have put the index *after* it because the end index is exclusive. The 'step" will begin at the starting index, and because it is set to "2," it will give us every second item: Monday, Wednesday, and Friday.

When you slice an object like a list or tuple, nothing happens to the original object. Our "weekdays" list is still intact, but now we have a new "class-days" list.

Data Manipulation
Appending Data
Because lists are mutable, you can add to them using the "append()" method. For instance, if you had a grocery list and you needed to add items to it, you could do this:

```
fruits = ["oranges", "apples", "cherry"]
```

```
fruits.append("grapes")
```

Modifying Data

Because lists have indices, you can modify items at a given index in your list. For example, let's say that in our fruits list, we don't want cherries, we want strawberries. In our code we could do this:

```
fruits = ["oranges", "apples", "cherry"]
```

```
fruits[2] = "strawberries"
```

Removing Data

To remove something from a list, there are two options: "`remove()`," or "`pop()`." The "remove" method will remove a specific list element while "pop" will remove an item at a given index.

```
fruits.remove("apples") or fruits.pop(1)
```

Notice that we've only been talking about manipulating lists. With tuples that is not possible. If we tried the "remove" or "pop" methods with our "weekdays" tuple, we'd get an error and that's because tuples are immutable. They are meant to remain constant throughout your code and for some collections, that is what you want.

Section 2: Dictionaries and Sets

Like tuples, dictionaries and sets are indexed using keys for easily retrieving information from complex data sets. They are also crucial to complex data organization.

Exploring Dictionaries and Sets

What Are Dictionaries?

Dictionaries are a data structure that stores information in key-value pairs. Unlike lists or tuples, dictionaries are not ordered. It's not necessary since you can retrieve what you need from a dictionary using a key rather than an index. The keys in the key-value pair must be unique but the data in a key-value pair can be of any type. One dictionary can have multiple data types inside it. Another important fact about dictionaries is that they are mutable, meaning they can be changed after being created.

What Are Sets?

Sets are collections of *unique* elements. Like dictionaries, sets are mutable. To add to a set you use the "add()" function. To remove something from a set you use the "remove()" function. Also, like dictionaries, sets can contain multiple data types – as long as the data types themselves are immutable. So, you can have strings, numbers, and tuples in a set because those types are immutable, but you cannot have other sets or lists in a set because those data types are mutable.

Sets are not ordered, they do not have an index, and they do not have key-value pairs. So, you cannot access an individual member of a set. What you *can* do is check if something is a member of a set.

```python
my_set = {1, 2, 3}

if 2 in my_set:

    print("2 is in the set")
```

The strength of a set is its ability to enforce uniqueness. For example, if you tried to create this set:

```python
my_set = {1, 2, 2, 3}
```

Python would still compile the code without error, but the set object would automatically exclude the duplicate "2" so that the set would only contain {1, 2, 3}.

Using a Dictionary.

Let's create a small contact management system using dictionaries. In our contact management system, we want to keep track of students. So, we have their name, email, phone, and GPA. We want to manage several student records, so the plan is to make a dictionary of dictionaries. So, that means I'll have an outer dictionary and an inner one. For the outer dictionary, we'll use student IDs for the key. The value attached to the key will be the dictionary holding each student's information.

```
1    # contact management example
2    student_info = {
3        1:{
4            "name":"Alice", "phone":"555-234-6789", "email":"alice@my_email.com","GPA":3.75
5        },
6        2:{
7            "name":"Joan", "phone":"555-234-7523", "email":"joan@my_email.com","GPA":2.90
8        },
9        3:{
10           "name":"Nick", "phone":"555-234-0845", "email":"nick@my_email.com","GPA":4.0
11       },
12       4:{
13           "name":"Bob", "phone":"555-234-5019", "email":"bob@my_email.com","GPA":2.45
14       }
15   }
```

To declare a dictionary, you just need a pair of curly braces and some key-value pairs. In our example, the outer dictionary is simply `{student_ID:student_dictionary}`, where the student ID is the key and the student's data, in dictionary format, is the value. The keys in our example are just single digits, but they could just as easily have been 6 digits or a string or even a tuple! As long as each key is unique, and they are an immutable data type, it doesn't matter.

What if I want to get the information for a specific student? All I need to know is the student's ID.

```
17    # Accessing student_info using IDs
18    student_id = 2
19    if student_id in student_info:
20        student_data = student_info[student_id]
21        print(f"Name: {student_data['name']}")
22        print(f"Email: {student_data['email']}")
23        print(f"Phone: {student_data['phone']}")
24        print(f"GPA: {student_data['GPA']}")
25    else:
26        print(f"Contact with ID {student_id} not found.")
```

Line 18: I am providing a student ID.

Line 19: The "if" statement checks to see if the ID is a member of the dictionary. If True, it pulls the data requested. If False, it says the student is not found.

Line 20: Because the ID provided is valid, a 'student_data" object is created from the dictionary associated with ID 2, and that information is printed.

Using A Set

If you're a school, you have lots of students and those students need IDs to keep their records straight. So, how do you keep from issuing duplicate IDs? One way you can do that is by using a set. With a set, you can see if an ID has already been issued so when you add a new student, you don't give them a duplicate by mistake.

Let's use some very simple code to demonstrate this.

```
28    # student ID check:
29    student_ids = {1,2,3,4}
30
31    new_id = 5
32
33    if new_id not in student_ids:
34        student_ids.add(new_id)
35        print(f"ID {new_id} added!")
36    else:
37        print(f"ID {new_id} already exists. Please try again.")
```

You'd want something more robust than this, but this gives you an idea of how a set can be used to enforce uniqueness. Just like in our dictionary example, this code uses an "if" statement to see if the ID we are adding already exists in the 'student_ids" set. If False, the ID is added. If True, the ID is excluded.

Section 3: Working with Files

Python's File-Handling Capabilities

In Chapter 3 where we discussed return statements, we used a coding example that imported Python's "CSV" module and showed how it could read from an external file. In addition to reading from files, Python can also write create, copy, move, and delete them. Knowing how to use these Python powers is an essential part of your programming arsenal. We'll dive into them here by building a simple file management tool.

File Management Example

Step One: Create a File

If you want to follow along, create a file called "file_mgr.py."

Step Two: Import Python Modules

```
1    import os
2    import shutil
3
```

The "os" module is Python's operating system module and allows Python to work with your system's OS. It allows Python to check for the existence of files and directories and to handle file-related tasks.

The second import, 'shutil," is Python's shell utility this module includes high-level file-handling capabilities such as copying and moving files among other things.

Step Two: Define the Menu, Part 1

```
4    def main_menu():
5        print("File Management Tool")
6        print("1. Copy a file")
7        print("2. Move a file")
8        print("3. Delete a file")
9        print("4. Exit")
10       choice = input("Enter your choice (1/2/3/4): ")
```

This function will respond to user input and give the user four options.

Step Three: Define the Menu, Part 2

```
12       if choice == '1':
13           copy_file()
14       elif choice == '2':
15           move_file()
16       elif choice == '3':
17           delete_file()
18       elif choice == '4':
19           print("Goodbye!")
20           exit()
21       else:
22           print("Invalid choice. Please select 1, 2, 3, or 4.")
23           main_menu()
```

Based on the user's choice, the code will perform one of three file actions, or exit the program.

Step Four: Define the File Copy Function

```
25    def copy_file():
26        source_file = input("Enter the path of the source file: ")
27        destination_folder = input("Enter the path of the destination folder: ")
28
29        if os.path.isfile(source_file) and os.path.isdir(destination_folder):
30            shutil.copy(source_file, destination_folder)
31            print("File copied successfully.")
32        else:
33            print("Invalid source file or destination folder.")
34
35        main_menu()
```

Lines 26-27: This asks the user for a source and destination file path. Ideally, you want to give the user a point-and-click option rather than a manual option like this, but this will do for now.

Line 29: This uses the "os" module to check if the user's entries are correct. The first part of the "if" statement checks to see if the file path entered points to a file. If either the path or the filename is incorrect, it will evaluate to "False." The second part of the "if" statement checks the path of the destination folder. If it is incorrect, it, too, will evaluate to "False." Because the statement uses the "and" logical operator, both parts of the statement need to be "True." If they are not, a message prints, and the user is sent back to the main menu.

Line 30: Using the 'shutil" module the user's file will be copied from the source directory to the destination directory. After printing a success message, the code returns the user to the main screen.

Step Six: Define the Move File Function

```
37    def move_file():
38        source_file = input("Enter the path of the source file: ")
39        destination_folder = input("Enter the path of the destination folder: ")
40
41        if os.path.isfile(source_file) and os.path.isdir(destination_folder):
42            shutil.move(source_file, destination_folder)
43            print("File moved successfully.")
44        else:
45            print("Invalid source file or destination folder.")
46
47        main_menu()
```

This operates much the same as the "copy_file" function except that this one *moves* the file from one location to the other.

Step Seven: Define the Delete File Function

```
49    def delete_file():
50        file_to_delete = input("Enter the path of the file to delete: ")
51
52        if os.path.isfile(file_to_delete):
53            os.remove(file_to_delete)
54            print("File deleted successfully.")
55        else:
56            print("Invalid file path.")
57
58        main_menu()
```

This works similarly to the previous two functions, only the "if" statement is different because it only needs to check for the existence of the file at the location provided.

Keeping the Menu Available
Here we're introduced to a bit of code we have not seen yet.

```
60    if __name__ == "__main__":
61        while True:
62            main_menu()
```

Line 60: The "if" statement uses a built-in Python variable: "__name__". (That's 2 underscores on either side of "file." The same is true for "main.") The statement is checking to see if the current script is running as the main program. If it is, the "__name__" variable is set to "__main__". If this script is being used as an import, then the "__name__" variable is set to the name of the script/module.

Line 61: When we discussed loops (Chapter 2), we said that an infinite loop is a bad thing, in this case, it's not – kind of like when we tell our kids it's bad to accept candy from strangers unless it's Halloween, then somehow it's OK to go out in the dark and accept candy from people you don't even know. Anyway, when it comes to displaying a menu, you want an infinite loop so the user can go back to it. This is why Line 61 has a "while" set to "True". "While" loops run until a condition is "False". In this case, we are forcing the condition to be "True". So, how does it end? It ends when the user explicitly ends the program. In an app with an interface, that would mean hitting a "close" button or clicking the "X" on the UI. Or, as in our example, giving the user a "Close" option on the menu.

Project: The GUI Weather App
Now we're going to add the finishing touches to our weather app and run it! So, let's put in those last few steps.

Step Seven: Setting Up the AOI Endpoint
Add these lines of code to make the connection to the API.

```
45   # Set up the API endpoint for weather data
46   weather_api_url=
     "http://api.openweathermap.org/data/2.5/weath
     er"
```

Be very careful with the spelling:

weather_api_url=http://api.openweathermap.org/data/2.5/weather

Step Eight: Putting the Result Label on Our GUI

Here's where we'll take the results of the result_label widget we called

earlier and display it on the GUI.

```
48   # Label to display the weather result
49   result_label = tk.Label(window, text="")
50   result_label.pack()
```

Step Nine: Creating an Entry Field

Now we need to set up an entry field for the user to tell the app what

city's weather they want to see.

```
52   # Input field
53   # Entry label
54   location_label = tk.Label(window, text=
     "Enter a city:")
55   location_label.pack()
56
57   # Entry field
58   location_entry = tk.Entry(window)
59   location_entry.pack()
```

Step 10: Adding a Button and Keeping the App Open

Now add these last lines of code.

```
61    # Create a button for the user to fetch
      weather
62    fetch_button = tk.Button(window, text="Fetch
      Weather", command=fetch_weather)
63    fetch_button.pack(pady=10)
64
65
66    # Start the main loop to display the window
67    window.mainloop()
68
```

Line 62 builds the button, complete with a label.

Line 63 adds some padding below the button so that the GUI window does not end abruptly at the bottom edge of the button.

Running the App

OK, now for the fun part: running the app. In your IDE, you can open a terminal the command below and hit ENTER, or if you're using VSCode, you can go to the upper right of coding screen and click the "run" button.

py weather_app.py

Mac users might need to use "py3" instead of "py." Once the command is run, your weather GUI will appear and you can enter the name of a major city to get its weather. Try entering a nonsense string to see how it responds when you enter a place it cannot find. Enter "Narnia" or "Middle Earth" if you want the weather there. (Not kidding.)

Troubleshooting

If your code does not seem to be working, try these steps:

- Walk through the steps again and check your syntax. That would include spelling and indentations.

- Google the error message and include that this is for a Python error.

- Open ChatGPT drop in your code and ask it to analyze it.

Chapter 4 Recap!

Believe it or not, at this point in your programming journey you now have a good foundation to build on! We've just finished exploring data structures. In Chapter 5, We'll introduce you to the world of Object-Oriented Programming. It's a programming model that helps you take the building blocks you have now and design complex, organized, and reusable code. You've reached a coding milestone! Good on you! Now let's move on to the next phase of your journey!

CHAPTER 5: PYTHON AND OBJECT-ORIENTED PROGRAMMING

Being the powerful and versatile language that it is, Python, of course, supports Object-Oriented Programming (OOP). OOP is a programming paradigm that allows you to model real-world concepts as objects, hence the name "Object-Oriented Programming." It's probably a little unfortunate that OOP is one letter off from "oops," which is what happens when you make a coding mistake, but that's how it is.

Section 1: What is OOP?

"Object-oriented programming (OOP) is a programming paradigm in computer science that relies on the concept of classes and objects. It is used to structure a software program into simple, reusable pieces of code blueprints (usually called classes), which are used to create individual instances of objects. There are many object-oriented programming languages, including JavaScript, C++, Java, and Python." (Doherty, n.d.)

Python is not limited to OOP, it also supports procedural programming styles.

Section 2: The Building Blocks of OOP

OOP has four essential building blocks:

- Classes

- Objects

- Methods

- Attributes

Classes

Classes are user-defined data types (Doherty, n.d.). We touched on this in our weather app project. Another way to think of classes is to see them as blueprints for objects. For example, to build a house, you need a blueprint to know how to construct it.

Objects

Objects are instances built from classes. An instance is the house you build from your blueprint. You can build many houses from one blueprint. You can also create many instances from one class. Something to keep in mind is that you can build many houses from one blueprint, but they don't all have to look exactly alike. You can use different colors and other accents to make each house unique. How does that apply to instances? More on that later.

Methods

Methods are representations of actions in your class. To use a method with an object, you use "dot" notation. For the weather app, we did this:

```
# Create a window instance

window = tk.Tk()

# Set the window title

window.title("Weather Forecast App")
```

We created a "Tkinter" window object, then we called the "title" method to put a title on the app.

Attributes

Attributes, also referred to as fields, store data in your class. The state of an object is defined by its attributes. If we go back to our blueprint analogy, let's say you made a "house" class. With instance attributes (attributes that affect the individual instances of your class), you could have one called "self.color", and with that, you could make one instance of a house blue and another red.

Section 3: Inheritance and Composition

"Inheritance and composition are two major concepts in object oriented [sic] programming that model the relationship between two classes. They drive the design of an application and determine how the application should evolve as new features are added or requirements change.

"Both of them enable code reuse, but they do it in different ways." (Python, 2023)

The Inheritance Model

Inheritance models the "is a" relationship. It represents the relationship between a base class and any class that is derived from it. For example, let's say you have a base class called "Vehicle". In that class, you have some initial attributes such as year, make, and model. The class also has a method to start the engine and another to stop it. You can make a specific model of vehicle, So, you create a "Car" class derived from "Vehicle", meaning your car class has this relationship with the vehicle class: "Car" is a "Vehicle".

In our example, "Car" is referred to as a subclass, a derived class, or a subtype. The "Vehicle" class is referred to as a superclass, or base class. Our "Car" class is said to inherit, derive from, or extend the vehicle class. Because "Car" is derived from "Vehicle", it inherits the interface and implementation of "Vehicle". This means that your "Car" class has year, make, and model included and has access to the start and stop engine methods in the "Vehicle" class.

About Methods
Methods are essentially functions, but they live inside a class and are called using "dot" (.) notation.

About Class Names
In Python, classes use "camel case" for their names. This means class names always start with capital letters and if the class name is more than one word, the next word is capitalized with no spaces between it and the word preceding it. Example: ThisClassNameIsLong.

Composition
Composition models have a "has a" relationship. Let's go back to our car analogy. We derived the Car from the Vehicle class, but a car needs an engine. So, let's create a "Motor" class. The Car class is not derived from the Motor class. Instead, it uses the Motor class as a component because every car has a motor. In this relationship between the Car class and the

Motor class, Car is the composite class, and Motor is the component class. Logically, a car *is a* vehicle that *has a* motor.

Let's demonstrate this with some example code.

Vehicle Super Class Example

```
1    class Vehicle:
2        def __init__(self, make, model, year):
3            self.make = make
4            self.model = model
5            self.year = year
6
7        def start_engine(self):
8            print(f"The {self.year} {self.make} \
9                {self.model}'s engine is now running.")
10
11       def stop_engine(self):
12           print(f"The {self.year} {self.make} \
13               {self.model}'s engine has been stopped.")
```

In the example shown above, note that "\" is being used to break the lines to save page space. They can be removed if you are writing this in your own code.

Line 1: The class name. As mentioned before, class names in Python are capitalized and use "camel casing" for compound words.

Line 2: The "__init__" declaration has two underscores (_) on either side of it. The "__init__" definition is called automatically when a class is initialized and defines class attributes on initialization. This definition is referred to as the class's constructor since it is what the code uses to construct an instance of the class. In this example, the constructor is initializing the make, model, and year attributes. The "self" keyword is a reference to the specific instance. Think of it as the instance saying, "me", or "my".

Lines 3-4: This means that this class will accept inputs for these attributes when initialized.

Lines 7-9 and 11-13: These are the start_engine and stop_engine functions of the Vehicle class. When these functions are referred to outside of the Vehicle class, these very same functions are referred to as *methods.*

Car Subclass/Inheritance Example

The Car class is a subclass of Vehicle. It can also be called a "derived" class. It inherits the attributes of the Vehicle class by extending the Vehicle class.

```
26    class Car(Vehicle):
27        def __init__(self, make, model, year, \
28                     num_doors, engine):
29            super().__init__(make, model, year)
30            self.num_doors = num_doors
31            # Composition: Car has an Engine
32            self.engine = engine
33
```

Line 26: Note the word "Vehicle" inside the parentheses. This says that the Car class is extending the Vehicle class and therefore is inheriting its attributes.

Line 27-28: As in the previous example, this is the constructor for the Car class. It includes attributes for make, model, year, number of doors, and engine.

Line 29: The "super()" keyword refers to the superclass that Car is using. In this case, it means the Vehicle class. In parentheses, it has "make", "model", and "year". This means it will reflect whatever attributes were passed into the Vehicle class when it was initiated.

Line 30: This "num_doors" attribute is specific to the Car class. So, it is called using the "self" keyword and it will accept whatever is passed to it when it is initialized.

Line 32: The "engine" attribute is also unique to the Car class and demonstrates the idea of composition because it will get its engine attribute from another class (not shown yet) called "Motor."

The Car class continued:

```
34        def honk_horn(self):
35            print(f"The {self.year} {self.make} \
36                {self.model} beeps the horn.")
37
38        def start(self):
39            print(f"The {self.year} {self.make} \
40                {self.model}'s engine is starting.")
41            self.engine.start()
42
43        def stop(self):
44            print(f"The {self.year} {self.make} \
45                {self.model}'s engine is stopping.")
46            self.engine.stop()
47
```

There are three functions in the Car class. Note **Line 41** (and the similar notation in line 46). It is referring to itself, calling upon its "engine" attribute which will come from the "Motor" class that We'll see in a minute, and is using the "engine" object's "start()" method. That method is a function in the Motor class but as mentioned earlier, when a function is called from outside its class, it's referred to as a method.

Motor Component Class Example

```
15    class Motor:
16        def __init__(self, fuel_type):
17            self.fuel_type = fuel_type
18
19        def start(self):
20            print(f"The engine starts running on \
21                {self.fuel_type} fuel.")
22
23        def stop(self):
24            print("The engine has been stopped.")
25
```

Line 16-17: This is the Motor class's constructor, and it is initializing the fuel source attribute which can accept any type of fuel source given to it at initialization.

Lines 19-21 and 23-24: These are the start and stop functions of the Motor class.

Putting the Classes to Work

```
48    # Create Engine object for Car to use
49    engine = Motor("Gasoline")
50
51    # Create Car object and use engine component
52    car = Car("Ford", "Bazinga", 2031, 4, engine)
53
54    # Use the Car methods
55    car.start_engine()
56    car.honk_horn()
57    car.start()
58    car.stop()
59    car.stop_engine()
60
```

Line 49: Before the Car class can be used, a motor object needs to be initiated. This line creates a Motor object called "engine" and initializes with the fuel type of "Gasoline". The user could just as well have entered "diesel," "electricity," or "Mr. Fusion Reactor."

Line 52: With the "engine" object initialized, a "car" object can be initialized using the Car class and entering the needed attributes. The Vehicle class needs a year, make, and model to initialize and that is provided by the initialization of the Car class. The Car class also gets its remaining parameters with the inclusion of a number for the doors, and the engine object it got from the Motor class.

Lines 55-59: To test that everything works, this method calls to the "car" object and takes it for a spin.

Section 4: Modules and Libraries

Modules

Modular programming is a key concept in all modern programming languages. It is the practice of breaking your programming code into smaller, self-contained modules. For example, your car has a battery. The battery serves one function. It provides an electrical source for your vehicle. It might serve other more complex parts in your car, but the battery's function is simple and clearly defined. It provides power. In code-speak, we could say that when you put a battery in your car, you're importing a battery module to use in your car program. Not only that, but you can put a car battery in most cars. You don't have to buy a brand-specific car battery. They do the same thing regardless of the vehicle.

In Python, a module works in much the same way. It is just a file with a ".py" extension that contains statements and definitions. You have used modules in your coding projects. Whenever you used the "import" keyword you were importing a module. Python has a huge list of built-in imports located here:

https://docs.python.org/3/py-modindex.html

Because Python is open source, there are plenty more online and you can write your own as well.

The advantages of modules include:

- **Organization:** Modules help you to keep code organized by keeping things together by functionality.

- **Reusability:** Consider Python's "math" module. It has all kinds of math functions inside it and can be imported into any Python code requiring math functions. It is reusable and it keeps you from having to write math functions yourself.

- **Namespace Safety:** Modules, create separate namespaces for your functions and variables. It's very possible that a variable or function name included in one module could also be present in another. Thanks to "dot" notation, the potential conflict is minimized because to use a function from a module, the syntax is `module_name.function_name()`. So, even if two modules you were using both had a function called "walk_dog", you can specify which function you mean by using the module name in the function call.

- **Encapsulation:** Encapsulation allows a module to hide certain aspects of its operation and serves to make it easier for others to use. For example, to start your car, you just need to know how to turn the key in the ignition. You don't have to know about or explain the intricacies of the motor, the transmission, the brakes, etc. You can just use those things and not have to concern yourself with them.

Libraries

Libraries are simply collections of modules. Although they are not required to, libraries tend to have general themes. Some are general purpose like Python's Standard Library. Others are focused on machine learning or web development.

A Simple Code Example

I have two files in the *same* directory:
- test_my_module.py
- myModule.py

The "myModule.py" file has two functions in it. One adds two numbers and the other multiplies to numbers. In my "test_my_module.py," I import "myModule" and use the two methods from my import:

```
1 import myModule
2
3 print(myModule.add_two_nums(7,8))
4 print(myModule.multipy_two_nums(7,8))
```

When I run this, line 3 gives me the result of 15, and line 4 gives me the result of 56. The methods that did the work, were in the "myModule.py" module. There may be times when you need to create a custom module for actions that you do repeatedly throughout your code. The ability to create your own modules makes this possible and convenient.

The "myModule.py" file:

```
File  Edit  Format  Run  Options  Wind
1 def add_two_nums(x,y):
2     return x+y
3
4 def multipy_two_nums(x,y):
5     return x * y
```

Chapter 5 Recap!

In this chapter we looked at the building blocks of Object-Oriented Programming and how it is supported in Python. As part of our study of OOP, we looked at inheritance and composition and learned that inheritance models have an "is a" relationship and composition models have a "has a" relationship. (A car is a vehicle, and it has a motor.) Finally, we looked at modules and libraries and learned how modules can help you organize code into reusable and convenient units that you can use across all kinds of code like how a car battery can be used in lots of different cars.

But as every seasoned programmer will tell you, it's hard to program things that are completely error-free. The more complex your code becomes, the more error checking you'll have to do, and that's to say nothing of the ways your users will find ways to break your code. So, in chapter 6 We'll dive into another important aspect of writing code and that is debugging and decoding. See you there!

CHAPTER 6: DEBUGGING AND TROUBLESHOOTING

The term "computer bug" refers to a real-life insect. "The first recorded instance of a bug causing a technical malfunction occurred in 1947 when engineers working on the Mark II Aiken Relay Calculator, an early computer at Harvard University, found a moth lodged in the machine's hardware." (Old, 2023)

> *"Debugging is removing the bugs from your program.*
> *Programming is the practice of putting them in." –*
> *Unknown*

Ideally, you *don't* want bugs in your code, but try as you might, they can still show up, appearing out of nowhere, like gnats in summertime. It might come in as a typo you didn't catch. It might show up as a scenario you didn't plan for. It could even be frustratingly random. Part of writing code is debugging and troubleshooting and, in this chapter, that's what we are going to look at.

Section 1: Identifying and Understanding Common Python Errors

This is not an exhaustive list, but these are some of the most common Python coding errors.

Syntax Errors.

Syntax errors are a common problem for beginning programmers. You'll find as you become more proficient in writing code, you'll have fewer syntax errors. Here is a very common example:

```
1  if x = 10:
2      print('X is equal to 10')
3
```

So, what's the problem? In Line 1 an *assignment* operator is being used in place of a *comparison* operator. Line 1 is attempting to assign the value of 10 to "x". You cannot do that in an "if" statement. What's needed here is a double-equals (==) to essentially ask the question: "Is the current value of x equal to 10?" Here's what the code should look like:

```
1  if x == 10:
2      print('X is equal to 10')
3
```

Indentation Errors

If you've been writing the code in this book as you've been reading, you should be a pro at this. Because Python emphasizes readability, it enforces strict rules on things like indentation. Here's an example of an indentation error:

```
1    # Print numbers from 1 to 10
2    for i in range(1, 11):
3    print(i)
```

Python will see this as an incomplete "for" loop because the print statement underneath it is not indented. This is the correction:

```
1    # Print numbers from 1 to 10
2    for i in range(1, 11):
3        print(i)
```

Let's modify this to show another indentation problem:

```
1    # Print numbers from 1 to 10
2    for i in range(1, 11):
3        print(i)
4
5    if i % 2 == 0:
6        print(f "{i} is even.")
```

At first glance, this appears to be correct. Both statements are indented correctly when viewed by themselves. However, the "if" statement will throw an indentation error because it is not indented below the "for" loop. The correct syntax should be:

```
1   # Print numbers from 1 to 10
2   for i in range(1, 11):
3       print(i)
4
5       if i % 2 == 0:
6           print(f "{i} is even.")
7
```

Naming Errors

Naming errors occur when you try to use a function that has not been declared. Here is a simple example:

```
1   x = my_func(3,4)
2   print(x)
3
```

If you were to try to run this code, it would throw an error because the function "my_func" has not been defined yet.

Type Errors

Type errors occur when you try mixing types. For example, you try to add the string representation of a number to an actual number.

```
1   result = 5 + "3"
2   print(result)
```

This will throw a type error because the code is trying to add (or concatenate) the number 5 to the string "3". There are two possible solutions to this depending on what outcome you want.

This will add and give you the number 8:

```
1    result = 5 + int("3")
2    print(result)
```

This will concatenate and give you the string "53":

```
1    result = str(5) + "3"
2    print(result)
```

Index Errors

Index errors occur when you try to access an index in something like a list and you request an index that is out of bounds, meaning you are trying to access an index that does not exist. Consider this example:

```
1    my_list = [1,2,3,4]
2    print( len(my_list))
3    print(my_list[4])
```

This is because indexes always start with zero and index 4 is out of range. To get back the number 4 from "my_list" I would need index 3:

```
1    my_list = [1,2,3,4]
2    print( len(my_list))
3    print(my_list[3])
```

To see the length of a list, you can use the "len" function as shown in line 2 and remember that the last available index would be one less than the length of your list.

Key Errors

Key errors are like index errors. Where index errors occur when you try to access a non-existent index, key errors occur when you try to access a non-existent key in something like a dictionary. Here's an example:

```
1  my_dict = {'first name': 'John',\
2          'last name': 'Jingleheimerschmidt'}
3  print(my_dict['middle name'])
```

The correct version of this code would look like this:

```
1  my_dict = {'first name': 'John',\
2          'last name': 'Jingleheimerschmidt'}
3  print(my_dict['last name'])
```

Attribute Errors

Attribute errors happen when you try to access an object attribute in the wrong way, or you try to access an attribute that does not exist in the object. Going back to our list example, let's say you wanted to add the number 5 to it.

```
1  my_list = [1,2,3,4]
2  my_list.add(5)
3  print(my_list[4])
```

This will not work because you cannot use "add" to add another item to a list. Instead, you need to use the "append" attribute.

```
1    my_list = [1,2,3,4]
2    my_list.append(5)
3    print(my_list[4])
```

As you become more proficient in your use and understanding of Python, you'll likely commit fewer and fewer of these kinds of errors. Now that you understand what they are and how to fix them, you can become more confident in your Python programming skills.

Section 2: Systematic Troubleshooting Strategies

Isolate the Problem

Look at the symptoms. Part of troubleshooting is a bit like a doctor interviewing a patient. Start by understanding the problem symptoms such as:

- Error messages

- Unexpected behavior

- Incorrect output

Narrow the problem down. See if you can identify the problem to a specific part of your code.

- Troubleshooting 101: Find out when the problem started happening. Has it been an issue from day one, or did it start after a change in the code or a change in how the code was being applied? Knowing the history of a problem can go a long way toward pinning it down.

- What are the error messages telling you? Sometimes they can pinpoint the location of the problem.

- Break your code into smaller pieces and test them individually. For instance, if you have identified a particular function (or functions) to be part of the issue, try to put them into a separate piece of code, feed it the parameters it needs and see how it responds.

Reproduce the Issue

Like the above, create a simplified version of your code, removing as many unrelated parts as possible. What you want is a minimized, functioning version of your program that focuses on the problem pieces. With that, you want to reproduce the problem so you can identify the root cause.

Do a Code Walk-through and Check Inputs and Outputs

Visually and verbally go through your code and pay attention to the inputs and outputs. When I say, "verbally," I literally mean talk your way through your code and explain what it's doing. For this step, it helps to have someone there to whom you are explaining your code because doing that forces you to step outside of your work and look at it objectively. You will be surprised how often using that technique helps you see things you missed.

Use Version Control

If you're using a version control system like Git, revert to a previous version of the code before the issue started. Create a separate branch and slowly reintroduce changes until you see the problem re-emerge. This will also help you to isolate the issue and correct it.

Use Print Statements to Trace Program Flow

I suppose you can call the use of print statements "the poor man's debugger," but it is a quick and effective way to spot problems in your code. The process is simple:

Use Strategically Placed Print Statements

- Print variables, and intermediate results at key points in your code.

- Use the type() function to print the classes of variables and results where needed.

- Include clear descriptions to identify where in the code you are so you can find fail points more easily.

Use Conditional Printing

This means using conditional statements that only print when certain conditions are met. This is especially helpful in scenarios where you are expecting a certain behavior to occur (or not occur) and the program is not responding as expected.

Use the Debugger Console

If you're using an IDE to develop your code, you can use the debugger console to help you see what is going wrong.

Read the Error Messages

Tracebacks

In Python, a traceback is a report that shows what caused an exception to occur. A traceback typically includes the following information:

- **Error Type and Message.** This includes the type of exception that occurred (TypeError, NameError, etc.), and a message describing the error.

- **File and Line Number.** This is very helpful in helping you pinpoint where your code went off the rails. The message will tell you what file the error occurred in and on what line number. Both are valuable pieces of information.

- **Function Calls.** This tells you what function call(s) led up to the error.

Google the Error

Sometimes the fastest way to figure out how to handle an error is to use Google. For best results, copy the error message and paste it into your Google search. Chances are, someone else has run into the same or similar situation.

Use ChatGPT

What is helpful with ChatGPT is its ability to understand human inputs and respond in a human-friendly manner. As intelligent as it is, it always helps to give it a context. For example:

"I am writing Python code for a weather app, and it keeps giving me this error: [INSERT ERROR MESSAGE HERE]. My code is below. Can you tell me what is wrong with it?

[INSERT YOUR CODE]"

ChatGPT will analyze your code, identify the problem, and often offer corrections. The more detail you provide, the better your results.

Consult the Documentation

You can find Python's official documentation here:

https://docs.python.org/

If the error you are dealing with involves the use of a Python keyword or built-in function, this documentation will explain how the function should be used and often offers examples of correct use.

Ask for Help

There are plenty of sites and community platforms that are dedicated to Python. Just be sure to provide a clear description of the issue, any relevant code snippets, and an explanation of what you are trying to accomplish with your code.

Sample Debugging Scenario

Let's say we've designed a function that averages a list of numbers.

```
1   def calculate_average(numbers):
2       total = 0
3       count = 0
4
5       for number in numbers:
6           total += number
7           count += 1
8
9       average = total / count
10      return average
```

There's nothing wrong with our function. But now someone tries to use our code and enters a list like this:

```
13   data = [10, 20, 30, 40, 50, "60"]
14   result = calculate_average(data)
15   print(f"The average is: {result}")
```

The problem is obvious just by looking at the code. The list includes 60 as a string rather than a number. But for the sake of this scenario, let's run it and see the result.

```
18   Traceback (most recent call last):
19     File "...", line 14,
20       in <module>
21       result = calculate_average(data)
22               ^^^^^^^^^^^^^^^^^^^^^^^^
23     File "...", line 6,
24       in calculate_average
25       total += number
26   TypeError: unsupported operand type(s) for +=: 'int' and 'str'
```

This is the traceback message I got from the VSCode terminal window. (The lines in this example have been wrapped to fit the page.)

Line 19 shows that the error occurred in the function call at line 14 in the code. It also shows what file the error occurred. This is especially helpful if your code references multiple files.

Line 21 shows the actual function call.

Line 25 shows the line in the function where the error happened.

Line 26 shows the error type and explains what the problem is: there is a string where an integer is expected.

At first glance, it looks like the problem is in the "calculate_average" function. However, when you look at the error type, you can see that the problem is not with the function but with the data it's receiving. From there you would know to check where the function call occurred (line 21) and look at what data was being passed in. As we said above, when you look at the list being passed in, there is a string where there should be an integer.

This is a very simple debugging example, but it demonstrates the debugging process and shows you how traceback messages can help identify problems in your code.

Section 3: Debugging Tools

Integrated Development Environments

Most IDEs have built-in debugging tools. Most of the code screenshots in this book come from Visual Studio Code, my IDE of choice. For shots where I don't want IDE markups to clutter the view, I am using Notepad++.

Python's IDE called IDLE also has some built-in debugging, but it is limited. Other IDEs that include debuggers include PyCharm and Thonny.

Print Statements

We already covered this in a previous section, but using print statements is also a form of debugging. Even with a built-in debugger, print statements can be helpful since they are quick and easy to use.

Logging

Python has a "logging" module that provides a flexible way to track your code's progress and provide messaging akin to using print statements but more structured. Here is an example showing how to set up logging in your code:

```
1   import logging
2
3   # Configure logging
4   logging.basicConfig(
5       level=logging.DEBUG,
6       format='%(asctime)s - %(levelname)s - %(message)s',
7       filename='example.log'
8   )
```

Line 1: This imports the logging module.

Line 4: "logging.basicConfig" as the name suggests, allows you to gather some basic logging information.

Line 5: Because this example demonstrates the debugging feature of logging, the level is set to "DEBUG". Here is a list of the available levels:

- **DEBUG** (10): This provides detailed information for diagnostic purposes and is typically used for testing and debugging.

- **INFO** (20): This gives general information and lets you know if things are running as expected. If constant monitoring of your app is needed, you can use this as a means of verifying that your code is performing as it should.

- **WARNING** (30): This is used to show that there is an issue that might need further investigation but is non-fatal. In other words, your code will still work but there may be fixes needed.

- **ERROR** (40): This indicates an error that requires attention. Depending on how your code is designed to respond to a particular error, your code can be set to stop, or it can continue but require attention.

- **CRITICAL** (50): This indicates an error that could stop your application from running and requires immediate attention.

Each of these settings has a corresponding number and the numbers can be used instead of the word, but the use of the word makes for clearer code (in my opinion). The other thing to understand about these numerical levels is that each level will only display messages at that level or above. So, INFO will show INFO messages and everything above it, but it will NOT show DEBUG messages.

Line 6: This allows you to configure the format of the log messages produced.

Line 7: If you want the log saved to a file, this setting allows you to set the file name.

To use logging in your code, you follow a syntax similar to using a print statement. (See lines 12 and 14 below.)

```
10    # Some example functions
11    def add_numbers(a, b):
12        logging.debug(f"Adding numbers: {a}, {b}")
13        result = a + b
14        logging.info(f"Result: {result}")
15        return result
```

Python's Debugging Features

To use Python's built-in debugger, you need to import the Python Debugger (pdb) module.

```
1    import pdb
```

Once you have done that, you can set one or more breakpoints in your code. This will tell the debugger to start the debugging process.

```
 9  def main():
10          pdb.set_trace()
```

When the debugger starts you can then use these console commands to control the debugger's behavior:

- **"n" (next):** This will execute the current line and then stop at the next line in the function.

- **"s" (step):** This will step through the current line of code, stopping where possible in called or current function.

- **"c" (continue):** It will continue code execution until the next breakpoint, if any. Otherwise, it will allow the code to run until the code is finished.

- **"p" variable:** This will print the value of the specified variable. The syntax for this is p [variable name]. If you use the "p" command without a variable, it will give the value of the last evaluated expression.

Section 4: Best Practices to Minimize Debugging and Troubleshooting.

At the beginning of this chapter, I pretty much said that bugs in your code are inevitable. To some extent, they are. But that doesn't mean we cannot strive to write bug-free code. So, in the interest of writing clean code that is debug-friendly, here are some valuable tips.

Use Meaningful Variable Names:

While you don't want to be too wordy, you also don't want to be so minimalist in your coding as to be cryptic. When you write your code and create variable names, remember the coder who has to come behind you to troubleshoot it, or add new features. That coder might be you! If another coder *does* have to pick up where you left off, be that person where everyone says: "They really wrote clean code!" Don't be the person where everyone says: "Fix *their* code? It'd be easier to start from scratch!"

Also, avoid single-letter variable names except where it's standard practice such as in loops.

Modularize Your Code

As much as possible, break your code into modular functions or classes. When you write your code, think in terms of reusability. Of course, there are lots of situations where the code you're writing is very project-specific, but even in projects like that, there is an opportunity to write code that can be used elsewhere. Also, by following a modular approach to your coding, you're doing yourself and others a favor because modularized code makes for easier debugging, troubleshooting, and maintenance.

Document Code Effectively

If you have ever read the Lemony Snicket book series called *A Series of Unfortunate Events*, you might remember *The Reptile Room* where Aunt Josephine writes a page full of "Nevers" to warn the Baudelaire children of potential dangers.

If I could get away with it, I'd write a page full of the words "Document! Document! Document!" Because I cannot emphasize enough how important code documentation is. I know that for programmers under pressure to produce code and meet deadlines, documentation sounds like a luxury, but code documentation is a huge time-saver in the long run. You'd be surprised how many times you return to your *own* code and wonder, "What was I thinking?" It's even worse for others looking at code someone else wrote.

Include comments to describe the purpose of functions in your code. Include comments within those functions that describe actions that are not obvious. Include a comment at the top of your code to explain the overall purpose of the file and its functions. Even describe assumptions, potential issues, and future plans.

Write Unit Tests
Automate your unit testing as much as possible. Just be sure to include unit tests to catch issues early in the development process.

Chapter 6 Recap!
In this chapter, we covered the very important topic of debugging and troubleshooting code. Of course, our goal is to make our code bug free to begin with, but as we said at the opening of this chapter, debugging and troubleshooting are part of the programmer's life. In this chapter, we listed some common coding errors, how to identify them, and how to troubleshoot them. We also looked at various troubleshooting and debugging tools, from those included in IDEs to the debugger built into Python. In that section, we also discussed how to do troubleshooting, how to build debugging into our code, and how to understand traceback

messages. Then we ended with some best practices for writing code that is debug friendly and easy to troubleshoot.

In Chapter 7, we're going to dive into the world of web development in Python. We'll touch upon development basics, and how to use the web framework called Flask. By the time we're done, you'll have a simple weather application deployed to the web! See you in Chapter 7!

CHAPTER 7: WEB DEVELOPMENT IN PYTHON

n the 1931 classic *Frankenstein,* the defining scene is when Dr. Frankenstein's creation comes to life and he begins to shout, "It's alive! It's alive!" Turning your code from concept to reality and seeing it work like you planned is a little like that. You run your code, it works, and you think: "It's alive! It's alive!" There's just a certain sense of satisfaction that comes from writing successful code. Yet as exciting as that is, now that "it's alive," the next step is to release it into the world. OK, I know, it didn't work out so great for the monster but that's fiction. Here, we're talking real code.

The focus of this chapter is to deploy your code to the web, but let's take a brief look at other ways to deploy your code.

You can see that classic *Frankenstein* scene here:

http://tinyurl.com/1931M

Section 1: Ways to Deploy Your Python Code

Python Library

If you've been following along in the book, you've already had experience with libraries. For some of our imports, we've used "pip install [library name]" to gain access to modules for us to use in our code. These installations pulled code libraries into our work. As you become more proficient with Python, you may find that you have scripts that you use frequently and that might be of use to others. Publishing your code as a code library is a great way to give back to the Python community. Going into the details of how to do this is outside the scope of this book, but if you want to pursue this, you can refer to this link:

https://realpython.com/pypi-publish-python-package/

Pros

Your code remains close to the original script and adds only what is needed to run it.

Cons

Your users will need to run your code with Python. The average user will not know how to do this. Others may not want to install Python on their device just to run your code.

Standalone Program

Turning your script into a standalone program is a more user-friendly approach to distributing your scripts. Your options include packaging your code or building a GUI (graphic user interface).

Packaging your code

There are several tools available for packaging your code. These include

- Briefcase

- py2app

- py2exe

- PyInstaller

Pros

Packaging your code eliminates most dependency issues. Your package includes an executable and any of its dependencies.

Cons

While packaging your code can simplify distribution, using your code can prove difficult for many. Your code will need to run from a command prompt. Many users will not be familiar with how to do that or will consider it too impractical when other apps they have can run using a GUI.

Building a GUI

A GUI, or graphic user interface, is familiar to most users. The average user already understands how to use an application in this way. Some of the packages that help you build a GUI for your app include:

- TKinter

- wxPython

- PySimpleGUI

Pros

A GUI makes your application accessible to a much broader audience.

Cons

Your users will need to figure out what version of your application will work on their OS, and they will have to download and install your program. While this is not a problem for most users, if your app needs to run on a particular version of a given OS, some users may have difficulty determining what OS version they have and could run into installation issues.

Python Web Application

The most popular way to deploy your Python app to a large audience is by turning it into a web application.

Pros

Deploying your code as a web-based app makes it platform-independent. Your code is run on a back-end server that does all the heavy lifting and simply shares the results in a protocol understood by all browsers. Since nearly every computer/device has a browser and an Internet connection, web-enabling your application means anyone with a browser can use your app with hardly any setup on their part.

Cons

Users must have an Internet connection and a browser. If a user is using an unsupported browser, they will have to use a more mainstream one to use your application.

Section 2: Let's Build a Web-Based Weather App!

While I encourage you to write the code for this application as you go, you can also download the completed files and put them in their designated locations as per the instructions given here. You can also download and just use them as a point of reference. The link is given at the end of the Answer Key section.

Step One: Create a Folder for your App

This will become your program's package. On my machine, I created a folder called: "WebWeather." You can make yours whatever you want.

In VSCode, open the folder you just created. You need to make sure you are in this folder for the remaining steps. If you are in some other development tool, make sure you are working from within the folder you have created.

Step Two: Create a Virtual Environment

Make sure you are in the folder you created in step one. Creating a virtual environment for you to work in allows you to develop your application and test it as though it were on the web.

Open a terminal window:

Open a terminal window by typing "CTRL + `" (without the quotes). The little symbol you see in the command is located just below the ESC key on most keyboards. Pay attention to the folder path you see when the terminal opens. Make sure it is in the folder you created in step one.

Create the environment:

Make sure you have a terminal window open in your folder from step one. Use one of the commands shown below based on your OS:

Windows: `py -m venv .venv`

Unix/macOS: `python3 -m vevn .venv`

When you run the command, you'll see a .venv folder inside the folder you created for this exercise.

Activate the environment:
From your terminal window, run the command below based on your OS: [Note there is a dot(.) before the venv in both the commands listed below.]

Windows: .venv\Scripts\activate

Unix/macOS: source .venv/bin/activate

When the environment is activated, you should see (.venv) in front of the prompts in your terminal window.

If you need to deactivate your virtual environment:
Just type "deactivate" in the terminal window (without the quotes). When you do, you should see the (.venv) disappear from the prompts in your terminal window. To reactivate it, just follow the activation steps shown above. You will not need to reinstall the virtual environment.

Step Three: Install Packages and Support Files/Folders
Three packages must be installed for our app to work. In the past, we have installed one package at a time. With the command below, we are going to install three packages at once:

- requests

- python-dotenv

- Flask

Open a terminal window if you have not already (CTRL + `), make sure you are in the folder you created in step one, *activate your virtual environment* if you have not done so already, then run this command:

```
pip install requests python-dotenv Flask
```

Note that there are spaces between each of the package names. When you run the command, you may see a prompt that recommends an upgrade for pip. It will look something like this:

```
[notice] A new release of pip is available: 23.2.1 -> 23.3.1
[notice] To update, run: python.exe -m pip install --upgrade pip
```

You can run the upgrade using the command shown in the prompt, or just use this:

```
py -m pip install -U pip
```

That's how all the cool kids run the upgrade. Note that the "U" in that command is UPPERCASE. It's shorthand for "upgrade." When the installation completes, it will show the new version number above the command prompt.

Requirements file

Since our goal is to deploy this application, we need a requirements file. To do this, run this command in your terminal window:

```
pip freeze > requirements.txt
```

The "freeze" is a subcommand in pip that lists all the packages installed in an application. The ">" (greater than) symbol is a redirect that instructs "freeze" to list all the packages in a text file. In our case, that is the "requirements.txt" file. When the command completes, you should see a "requirements.txt" file in your application folder. You can run this command again to update it if you install more packages.

Why is this important?

When you decide to deploy this into the world, the requirements.txt file will let your hosting service know what packages to install to make your application work. You won't have to do that yourself. It will happen in the background for you.

The .gitignore file

In this chapter, as part of our deployment process, we'll be sending our code into a GitHub repository ("repo"). When planning to do something like that, certain files do not need to be shared publicly. A .gitignore file is what you use to prevent certain files from being sent to GitHub. So, in VSCcode (or IDE of your choice), create a file called ".gitignore" (without the quotes). Also note that the file name is preceded with a dot (.). When you create the file in VSCode, you'll notice in the file explorer that it gets a special icon next to it. Inside this file, you want to add these two entries:

.venv

.env

The first one is the folder for our virtual environment. The second one is a file for holding environment variables. In our case, that's the API key for our weather application. Because both are in our .gitignore file, none of their content will be loaded into the online repository.

The .env file

In your application folder, create a file called ".env" (without the quotes), noting that this file's name also has a dot (.) at the beginning of it. As mentioned above, we will use this to hold our API key.

Adding OpenWeatherMap.org API Key

If you've been following along and building the weather app from the previous chapters, you already have an API key. If you don't have one, you can go to openweathermap.org and sign up for one – it's free. To add your API key to your .env file, just open it and add this line:

API_KEY= [YOUR_API_KEY]

Replace the brackets and everything inside them with your API key *without quotes around it.*

Support Folders

In your application folder create these two subfolders:

- static

- templates

Note: The name "templates" *must be plural*, not singular. This is important because Flask, the web framework we'll be using, will throw an error if this file is not named as shown above.

Inside the static folder create a subfolder called "styles".

CSS File

Inside the *styles* folder create a new file called "style.css". Discussion of CSS files, what they do, and how they work is outside the scope of this book, but there are plenty of resources online to answer those questions if you're curious. For now, just know that CSS files help with the "look and feel" of the pages for your web application. The code for our CSS file is below:

```css
1  * {
2      margin: 0;
3      padding: 0;
4      box-sizing: border-box;
5  }
6
7  .centered{
8      text-align:center
9  }
```

```css
10  body {
11      padding: 2rem;
12      background-color: #333;
13      color: whitesmoke;
14      min-height: 100vh;
15      display: flex;
16      flex-direction: column;
17      align-items: center;
18      gap: 2rem;
19      font-size: 2rem;
20  }
```

```
22   input, button {
23        font-size: 2rem;
24        padding: 1rem;
25        border-radius: 10px;
26   }
```

HTML Files

There are three HTML files that we will use for our application:

- index.html

- weather.html

- badweather.html

As with the CSS file, the discussion of what HTML pages do, etc. is outside the scope of this book. These files need to live inside the *templates* folder. The code for each is below:

Index.html

```
1   <!DOCTYPE html>
2   <html lang="en">
3   <head>
4       <meta charset="UTF-8">
5       <meta name="viewport" content="width=device-width,
        initial-scale=1.0">
7       <title>What's The Weather?</title>
8       <link href="{{url_for('static',
9       filename='styles/style.css')}}" rel="stylesheet" />
10  </head>
11  <body>
12      <h1>What's the Weather?</h1>
13
14      <form action="/weather">
15          <input type="text" name="loc" id="loc"
16          placeholder="Enter a city."/>
17          <button type="submit">Submit</button>
18      </form>
19  </body>
20  </html>
```

(Note: lines 5-6, 8-9, and 15-16 were wrapped to fit the page. They each should be a single line.)

Weather.html

```
1   <!DOCTYPE html>
2   <html lang="en">
3   <head>
4       <meta charset="UTF-8">
5       <meta name="viewport" content="width=device-width,
6       initial-scale=1.0">
7       <title>{{title}}</title>
8       <link href="{{url_for('static',
9       filename='styles/style.css')}}" rel="stylesheet" />
10  </head>
11  <body>
12      <h1>{{title}} Weather</h1>
13          <p><img src='https://openweathermap.org/img/wn/
14          {{icon}}@2x.png'></p>
15          <p>{{status}} and {{temp}} &deg</p>
16          <p>Feels like {{feels_like}} &deg</p>
17          <p>Wind speed {{wind_speed}} MPH</p>
18          <p>{{wind_dir}}</p>
19      <form action ="/weather">
20
21          <input type="text" name="loc" id="loc"
22          placeholder="Enter a city."/>
23          <button type="submit">Submit</button>
24      </form>
25  </body>
26  </html>
```

(Note: lines 5-6, 8-9, and 13-14 were wrapped to fit the page. They should each be single lines.)

Lines 15-18: The data in these lines come from the JSON data retrieved from our weather.py code (which we have not written yet).

Badweather.html

```
1    <!DOCTYPE html>
2    <html lang="en">
3    <head>
4        <meta charset="UTF-8">
5        <meta name="viewport"
6        content="width=device-width,
7        initial-scale=1.0">
8        <title>Bad Weather Request</title>
9        <link href="{{url_for('static',
10       filename='styles/style.css')}}"
11       rel="stylesheet" />
12   </head>
13   <body>
14       <h1>Bad Weather Request</h1>
15       <h2 class="centered">Could not
16       retrieve requested data.
17       <br>Please try again.</h2>
18       <form action ="/weather">
19           <input type="text" name="loc" id="loc"
20           placeholder="Enter a city."/>
21           <button type="submit">Submit</button>
22       </form>
23   </body>
24   </html>
```

(Note: lines 5-7, 9-11, 15-17, and 19-20 have all been wrapped to fit the page. They should each be single lines.)

Page Summary

Here is a quick summary of what each of these pages do:

The "index.html" page is the default page of web applications. When users use their browser to navigate to your page, it's the index.html page they see first. For our project, they will see a form where they will be asked to enter a city. In the background, our application will fetch the weather data using the API key and interpret that data in a user-friendly way.

The "weather.html" page will look very much like the index page, but it will be the page users will be transported to and where they will see the weather data they requested. It will also include a form where the user can enter *another* city to get weather information for their next choice.

The "badweather.html" page will handle bad requests. For example, the user enters a misspelling for a city, or they enter a zip code instead of a city name, or they enter a city that Open Weather does not recognize – or they enter gibberish. Rather than just dumping the user out of the app, our app will have some error handling built in that will take them to the "badweather.html" page where they will see a message saying the request could not be found and give them a form where they can try a different entry.

Special considerations
If you are familiar with HTML and CSS, you'll notice that the call to our CSS page looks a little unusual:

```
<link href="{{url_for('static',
filename='styles/style.css")}}" rel='stylesheet' />
```

This is because we are using Flask. We installed it earlier. Flask is a lightweight web framework designed for Python. It's not the only one. There are others available, but Flask is what we are using for this example. For Flask to see and use our CSS, we have to use its syntax.

On our forms, if you look at the action attribute, you'll notice that the action is "/weather".

```
<form action ="/weather">
```

We have not included it yet, but our weather code will be used to get the weather information our user has requested.

Step Four: Implementing our weather code.

If you've been following along with the weather app we built earlier, some of this will look familiar. The key difference between our earlier weather app and this one is that for our first one, we created a mini-GUI to display the weather results. For this web-based app, we're going to create a version of the weather app that will display to the console and that can also be used to display on our web page. The advantage of having the weather app display to the console is that it will show us JSON data that we can use in our web application.

Create a new file in the top level of your application folder.

Create a new file called "weather.py" and place this outside the subfolders you made earlier. In the VSCode File Explorer, it should be in the main folder. See the image below.

Import packages

Check your terminal window. Make sure you are in the folder for your application and that the virtual environment is activated.

Add these lines to the weather.py file:

```
from dotenv import load_dotenv
from pprint import pprint
import requests
import os
```

The dotenv import allows our app to access the .env folder. The requests import handles API requests. When you add these to your code, your IDE will probably flag them. This is because they have not yet been accessed by our code.

After the above imports, skip a line and add this:

```
Load_dotenv()
```

Your code should look something like this now:

```
1    from dotenv import load_dotenv
2    from pprint import pprint
3    import requests
4    import os
5
6    load_dotenv()
```

Create a module to get weather data:

```
 8     # This function will be called by the web app.
 9     def get_current_weather(loc):
10         request_url =
           f'http://api.openweathermap.org/data/2.5/weather?ap
           pid={os.getenv("API_KEY")}&q={loc}&units=imperial'
11         weather_data=requests.get(request_url).json()
12         return weather_data
```

Line 10: You'll notice that we are using the os function from the dotenv package to access the API key. Also, please note that line 10 is wrapped to fit the page. Your line 10 should be a single line of code.

Line 11: you'll notice the word "json." JSON (JavaScript Object Notation) is a data interchange format easy for both humans and machines to interpret. It allows different platforms to share data easily. In our case, Open Weather Map is sending data to our weather application. To do this, it is sending its information in JSON format which is a notation both applications can understand.

Line 12: This returns the JSON data that our web application will interpret for our use.

Console Display
You do not have to include lines 14-18 in your code. I have it in mine just as a note to myself to remind me why the code after the comment exists:

```
14
15
16
17
18
```

The reason this code is here is so that we can run the weather app without the web interface and see the JSON data our code is receiving.

```
19    if __name__ == "__main__":
20        print('\n*** Today\'s Weather Conditions ***\n')
21
22        # '.strip() removes leading and trailing white space.
23        loc = input("\nPlease enter a city: ").strip()
24
25        # This sets a default city in case the user leaves it blank
26        if not loc:
27            loc = 'Atlanta'
28
29        weather_data = get_current_weather(loc)
30
31        print("\n")
32        pprint(weather_data)
```

Line 19: There are two underscores (_) on either side of the name and main. This line checks to see if this code is running on its own or if it's been called from another module. If it is running as a standalone module, it will run the lines below it and display the weather data in the terminal window. Why do we want that? So, we can decide what we want our web app to display and how we want to display it.

Note that lines 20-32 are all indented underneath line 19. If this module is called from the web application, lines 20-32 do not even run. They only run if we are running this module by itself.

Line 23: This line has ".strip()" at the end of it to remove leading and trailing whitespace. For example, if the user copies and pastes their entry into the city field, they might also accidentally include whitespace. The addition of .strip() prevents a possible error before it even happens.

Lines 26-27: The user might hit the submit button before entering anything. If the "loc" variable is left blank, our code will throw an error. Line 27 provides a default location of "Atlanta." You can make that any major city of your choice.

Line 29: Just like our web form does, this line calls the "get_current_weather" function. However, instead of feeding this to a web page, it feeds the results to the console.

Line 31: This just adds a blank line on the screen.

Line 32: This line outputs the JSON data in human-readable format.

Test your module

Make sure you have your virtual environment activated. Check the terminal window and make sure you are in the folder for your application. If you are in VSCode you can click the run button in the top-right corner of the screen.

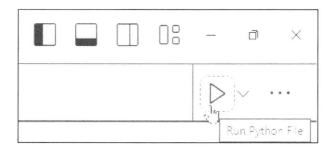

Or, in the terminal window, you can just run this command:

```
python weather.py
```

If everything is correct, you'll be prompted to enter a city and then you'll see your weather data. Also, try running it without a city to make sure it works that way as well.

```
*** Today's Weather Conditions ***


Please enter a city:


{'base': 'stations',
 'clouds': {'all': 100},
 'cod': 200,
 'coord': {'lat': 33.749, 'lon': -84.388},
 'dt': 1702821605,
 'id': 4180439,
 'main': {'feels_like': 43.23,
```

Step Five: Create a file to work with Flask.

Open a new file called 'server.py" and place that in your main application folder like you did the weather.py.

Next, we are going to add our code.

Make sure you have your virtual environment activated and that you are in the folder for your application.

Imports

We have several imports needed to support this module. The code is shown below.

```
1   from flask import Flask, render_template, request
2   from weather import get_current_weather
```

Also, on line one the "request" import is *different* from the "request" import we did earlier. The one you see on line one is unique to Flask.

Flask Code

This next line makes our app a Flask app:

```
5    app = Flask(__name__)
```

As mentioned before, the lines next to "name" are two underscores (_).

For Flask to find your web pages, you need to define routes. For a typical web page, a user can simply enter the web address in their browser, or they can enter the web address followed by \index.html. To cover both scenarios, we need to add two "@app" routes to our code:

```
7    .route('/')
8    .route('/index')
9    def index():
10       return render_template('index.html')
```

Below that, we tell Flask what to return in response (lines 9-10).

Proof of concept

Before we go into our full-blown weather app, we'll do a simple one just to demonstrate how this works. So, for now, comment out line 10 and make your code look like this:

```
 9    def index():
10        # return render_template('index.html')
11        return "This is your first python web app!"
```

Making the code a runnable module

This next section of code needs to **remain at the bottom of your code from this point forward.** You'll recognize this from the "weather.py" module. These lines make your module runnable.

```
13    if __name__ == "__main__":
14        app.run(host="0.0.0.0", port=8000)
```

This will allow your app to run on your local host, meaning that it will run on your machine like a web page. When you run it, you'll see a warning. That is normal. We will fix that later. For now, just run it by using the run button in VSCode, or by using this command:

python server.py

This is the warning you will probably see:

```
(.venv) PS C:\Users\htack\OneDrive\Programming\Python\webweather> python server.py
 * Serving Flask app 'server'
 * Debug mode: off
WARNING: This is a development server. Do not use it in a production deployment. Use a production WSGI server instead.
 * Running on all addresses (0.0.0.0)
 * Running on http://127.0.0.1:8000
 * Running on http://192.168.1.66:8000
Press CTRL+C to quit
```

"WARNING: This is a development server. Do not use it in a production deployment. Use a production server instead."

Below that, you will see two clickable web addresses. Click either one of them to see your web page. It should open in your default browser. You might also see a warning there as well. That is expected behavior. We will correct that shortly. If you cannot click the links in your terminal window, open a browser and enter this in the address bar:

```
Localhost:8000
```

Press ENTER and you should see your page displayed.

Go ahead and close the page, and then in the terminal window press CTRL + C to stop running on your localhost.

Fixing the warning

When you ran your proof of concept page, you got a warning about running on a development server. To fix this, we need to install another package. Again, make sure you have your virtual environment active and that you are in the folder for your application. Once you are sure of that, run this in your terminal window:

```
pip install waitress
```

Waitress will allow us to serve our application in production. Once that is installed, you'll need to update your "requirements.txt" file since you have installed a new dependency. So, in your terminal window run this command:

```
pip freeze > requirements.txt
```

If you open the requirements file now, you should see "waitress" listed as one of the dependencies. And now that we have it installed, let's add "waitress" to our imports:

```
from flask import Flask, render_template, request
from weather import get_current_weather
from waitress import serve
```

'serve" is what we will need to correctly serve our application. In our runnable module section, we'll need to make some changes as well:

```
13    if __name__ == "__main__":
14        serve(app, host="0.0.0.0", port=8000)
```

If you run this again, you will not see any prompts or instructions in the terminal window. To see if things are running properly, open a browser and enter localhost:8000 in the address bar, and press ENTER. You should again see your web page. Go ahead and close it and in your terminal window, press CTRL+C.

As mentioned before, from now on this should always be at the bottom of your server.py file:

```
13    if __name__ == "__main__":
14        serve(app, host="0.0.0.0", port=8000)
```

Everything else should be above these lines.

Now let's build our web-based weather app
Change line 10 back to what it was. You can delete what we had on line 11 earlier.

```
7     app.route('/')
8     app.route('/index')
9     def index():
10        return render_template('index.html')
```

The "get_weather" function
This section of code covers lines 12-33. (Your line numbers may differ.)
The code images shared are wrapped to get them to fit the page, so pay careful attention to wrapped lines when you put them into your code.

```
12    app.route('/weather')
13  ⊟def get_weather():
14  |     loc = request.args.get('loc')
```

Line 12: This tells Flask where to find the "weather" page. This is important because it's here where we're also defining our "get_weather" function.

Line 13: This opens the "get_weather()" definition. It is purposely named different from "get_current_weather()" to avoid any ambiguity in the code. The two definitions exist in different files, but they live in the same package (folder) so, giving each a distinct name avoids any namespace conflicts. Both you and your code are clear on which method you mean.

Line 14: This captures the location entered by the user.

As you start typing these next lines of code, your IDE is likely going to flag syntax errors. These will clear up as you follow along.

```
16        if not loc:
17            loc="Atlanta"
18        try:
19            weather_data = get_current_weather(
              loc)
20            return render_template(
21                'weather.html',
22                title=weather_data['name'],
23                status=weather_data['weather'][0
                ]['description'].capitalize(),
24                icon=weather_data['weather'][0][
                'icon'],
25                temp=f"{weather_data['main'][
                'temp']:.1f}",
26                feels_like=f"{weather_data['main'
                ]['feels_like']:.1f}",
27                wind_speed=f"{weather_data['wind'
                ]['speed']:.1f}",
```

Lines 16-17: These lines provide a default value for the "loc" variable in case the user presses ENTER without providing a value.

Line 18: This introduces a "try...except" block to handle errors. For example, if a user misspells a city name, or enters a city not covered by the API, it sends them to an error page that allows them to try again, instead of just dumping them out of the application.

Line 19: This calls the "get_current_weather" function from the weather.py module and passes in the location entered by the user.

Lines 20-29: These render the weather page with the JSON data gathered from the "get_current_weather" function.

Line 23: On this and line 24 you see this notation:

```
status=weather_data["weather"][0]["description"].capital
ize()
```

The 0 is there because we are accessing the first element in the weather section of the JSON data. The weather section of the JSON data looks like this:

```
'weather': [{'description': 'mist', 'icon': '50d', 'id': 701, 'main':
'Mist'}],
```

If you want to see this for yourself, you can run the weather.py file in the console. It's from this output that we are getting the information for the weather page.

Line 25: This line captures and formats the temperature data. The ".1f" formats the temperature out to one decimal place. You see the same notation in lines 26 and 27.

```
28              wind_dir=convert_direction(weather_data['     '][' ',])
29          )
30      except Exception as e:
31          return render_template(
32              '            '
33          )
```

Line 28: This calls another method to convert the wind direction. It passes in the data wind direction data as a value for the conversion method to interpret.

Lines 30-33: These close out the "try...except" section. If the user enters invalid information, they are redirected to the "badweather.html" page where they can try again.

```
35  def              (deg):
36      directions = ['  ','  ','  ','  ','  ','  ','  ','  ']
37      index = round(deg /  )%
38      direction = '              '
```

Line 35: This opens the definition for "convert_direction." It takes a number as an argument.

Line 36: This creates a list of directions that the function can return.

Line 37: This line calculates the direction to use from the list.

```
40      if directions[index] == 'N':
41          direction += 'North'
42      elif directions[index] == 'NE':
43          direction += 'the Northeast'
44      elif directions[index] == 'E':
45          direction += 'East'
46      elif directions[index] == 'SE':
47          direction += 'Southeast'
48      elif directions[index] == 'S':
49          direction += 'South'
50      elif directions[index] == 'SW':
51          direction += 'Southwest'
52      elif directions[index] == 'W':
53          direction += 'West'
54      elif directions[index] == 'NW':
55          direction += 'Northwest'
56      else:
57          direction = ''
58      return direction
```

This if...elif section builds the return statement from the direction calculation so that the user gets a compass direction for where the wind is coming from.

Ready to run!
Make sure you have your virtual environment activated and that you are in your application's directory. Once you have confirmed that, you can run this from VSCode by hitting the run button, or you can run this from the terminal window:

```
python server.py
```

When you do, the terminal window will give you no instructions. The cursor will just move down a line. To see your weather app in action, open a browser window, enter `localhost:8000` and press ENTER.

Experiment with large city names and try incorrect names as well to test the error handling. It should take you to the Bad Weather Request page and allow you to enter a new city.

After you have tested your web app, you can close the page, and stop the local host by pressing CTRL+C in the terminal window.

Step Six: Deploying to Git

This section will guide you through deploying your work to GitHub. You will need a GitHub account to do this. If you do not have a GitHub account, you will need to go to this site:

https://github.com/

From there, follow the prompts to open a free account. (You can also open a paid account if you prefer, but that is up to you.)

Installing Git on Your Machine:

Before attempting to install GitHub on your machine, check to see if you already have it.

Windows Users: Open a command prompt in administrator mode and at the prompt type this: `git version`. If you have git installed on your machine, it will show you what version of git you have installed. If you do *not* have git on your machine, you will see an error message of some kind stating that it is an unknown command.

If you do not have git installed, you can go here:

https://gitforwindows.org/

The installer will give you the latest version of git, which will include both the command line version and the GUI version.

Mac Users: Most MacOS versions already come with git installed. You can run "`git version`" (without the quotes) from the terminal to check. If you do not have git for some reason, you can also visit this site to download the latest version:

https://sourceforge.net/projects/git-osx-installer/files/git-2.23.0-intel-universal-mavericks.dmg/download?use_mirror=autoselect

Another recommended way to install git on a Mac is to go to this site and follow the installation instructions there:

https://sourceforge.net/projects/git-osx-installer/files/git-2.23.0-intel-universal-mavericks.dmg/download?use_mirror=autoselect

Initializing a local repo:

In a terminal window *inside your application folder*, run the following command:

```
git init
```

When you run this command your .env and .venv files should appear grayed out. If not, be sure to add them to your .ignore file. You want to do this because those files contain data you do not want to share publicly in GitHub when you go to deploy your code.

One other thing you want to add to your .gitignore file is the __pycache__ folder. (The folder name has two underscores on either side of it.) This folder is created automatically as you add modules to your application. It's not something you want to publish to GitHub.

Updating your repo:

Once you have everything in place and your .gitignore file up-to-date, it's time to add everything to your repository to get it ready for deployment to GitHub.

Adding your files to your repository

To add all your files to your local repo, run this command:

```
git add.
```

The dot instructs git to add all the files to your repo. When you do this, you'll notice that files with a "U" next to them (updated) will have an "A" next to them (added). You'll also notice that the files you added to your .gitignore file are ignored. There are no letters next to them.

Committing your files

The next step is to commit your files to the repository. To do that, run this command:

```
git commit -m "first commit"
```

The "-m" flag stands for "message" and it's a good idea to add a message to every commit you make so that you have a running commentary of every change you make. The message does not have to be super detailed, just enough detail to remind you what you did during a specific commit. After you run the command, you'll see a list of items that git committed to the repository.

Adding your files to GitHub:

To do this, you'll need to log into your GitHub account and create a new GitHub repo. This is where you'll be sending your local repo files.

Click New:

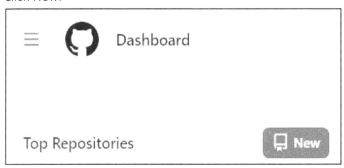

When you click "New," you'll come to a new screen where you'll see your account listed as the repo owner.

Choose a Repo Name

Under "Repository name," enter a name of your choice. If the name is available, GitHub will say so in green right under the name field. If for some reason the name you chose is not available, simply choose another.

Public or Private:

In the section below where you entered your repo name is the option to make your repo public or private.

If you have the option of marking it private, I recommend that you do so.

Create Your Repository

After you have completed the steps above, scroll to the bottom of the screen and click "Create Repository."

Capture the Git Command You Need

On the next screen that appears, scroll part way down to the section titled: "...or push an existing repository from the command line." You want this section because you've already run the other commands on your local repo.

In the right-hand corner, you'll see a copy icon.

Click that to copy the commands to your clipboard.

Run the Copied Commands

Now, go back to VSCode, or the IDE of your choice, and paste the commands into the terminal window. To do this in the VSCode terminal window, just RIGHT-CLICK inside it (CTRL+V will not work).

The first two of the three commands will run. It will pause on the third command and wait for you to hit ENTER. So, go ahead and do that.

Step Seven: Deploy to the Web

We're going to use Render.com to deploy our weather app to the web. You can set up a free account. We're using this because it can pull in your files straight from GitHub. To make things easier, I signed up using my GitHub account, but you have other options as well.

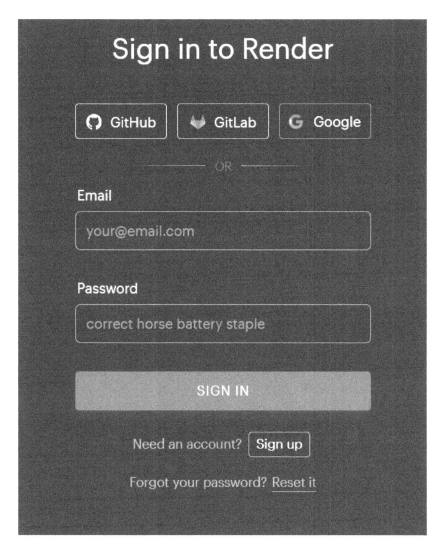

Start a New Web Service

After signing in, you'll come to the Render dashboard. Click the "New" button and choose "Web Service."

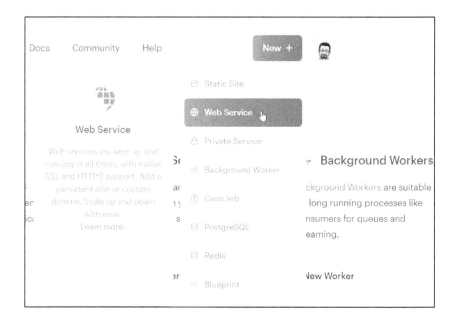

Import Your Files from Git

From the screen that appears, select "Build and deploy from a Git repository." Then click "Next."

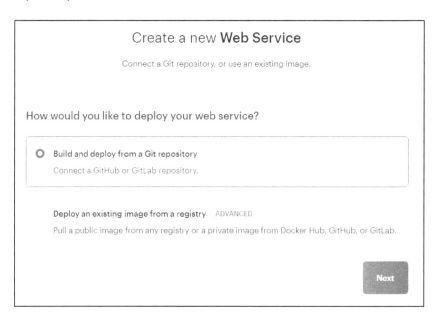

Connect Your Git Repository

On the following screen, you will be prompted to connect your GitHub account so you can pull in your files.

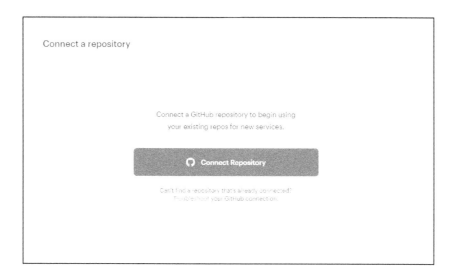

On the next screen, you will have the option to select all your GitHub Repositories, or just one. If you have multiple repos and you only want to use the one for this project, then use the "Only select repositories" option.

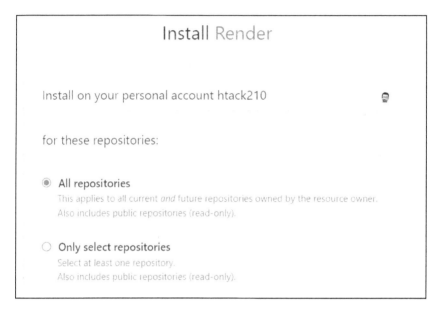

When you select the second option, you'll see a dropdown button where you can choose the repo you want to pull in.

After you select your repo, click "Install."

On the next screen, you will see your selected repo. Click the "Connect" button to continue.

Connect a repository

○ htack210 / PyWeatherApp · 2 hours ago   Connect

The next page presents you with several options. Fill these out as shown below:

Deployment Page

Name: You can have this match the name of your repo, or name it something else.

Region: You can leave this at its default or choose a region that is closer to you.

Branch: If your branch lives on the main branch (which is how the example is set up), you can leave this at "main." If you have your repo on a different branch, change it to that branch.

Root Directory: Leave as is.

Runtime: Python 3

Build Command: Change this to

```
pip install -U pip && pip install -r requirements.txt
```

This is to allow for pip to be upgraded if needed. The command after the "&&" updates the requirements.txt to include all the packages associated with your application.

Start Command: `python3 server.py`

This is how you would run this if you were running the app from inside the terminal.

Instance Type: Scroll down to see this section. I recommend that you use the free option.

Environment Variables: For us, this section is necessary because this is where we will include our API key. For "NAME_OF_VARIABLE" enter "API_KEY" (without the quotes). For "value" enter your API key (from the .env file).

You now need to click "Add Environment Variable" to add the version of Python you're using. For "NAME_OF_VARIABLE" enter "PYTHON_VERSION" (without the quotes). For "value" enter your Python version. To figure that out, go into your IDE and run this command in the terminal window:

```
py --version
```

Take *only* the version number shown and enter that as your value.

Once all this is in place, scroll to the bottom of the page and press "Create Web Service." The deployment will take a few minutes to complete. When the last line on the screen says, "Your service is live," you can open your site. The URL will be listed toward the top of the screen. You can click that and go straight to your new site.

Your web application is now on the web! Congratulations!

Chapter 7 Recap!

This has been a long and detailed chapter! If you put all the code in yourself, rather than just copying and pasting it in, good on you!

In this chapter, you learned a little about web frameworks. Granted, it was not in-depth, but you did get some exposure. If want to learn more about Flask or other web frameworks, there are plenty of resources available, especially on YouTube. Of all the ways to deploy your code, converting your code into a web app is probably the most popular and the most user-friendly.

In addition to using a web framework, you also learned some basic git commands. If you're going to be doing a lot of programming, learning how to use git is a worthy investment of your time. Whether you choose to use the GUI version of the command line version of git is up to you, but knowing how to use the command line version is probably the better choice in my opinion. Also, if you're interviewing for a programming job, saying that you are familiar with how to use git, is a point in your favor even if the place where you're interviewing uses some other kind of version control platform. It shows that you are familiar with the concept.

In Chapter 8 we'll dive into Python and data analysis where we'll cover using Pandas, data visualization, and how to put data analysis to practical use.

CHAPTER 8: DATA ANALYSIS AND VISUALIZATION

D ata analysis is a crucial part of programming, whether you're working for a large corporation and analyzing sales trends to determine future production forecasts, running your own business, and looking at customer trends to see what sells best, or engaged in scientific analysis working on the next great breakthrough. But raw data is of no value if you don't have a way to analyze it in a meaningful way. Because of its many powerful libraries, and its simplicity, Python is a popular choice for data analysis tasks.

As always, while I encourage you to write this code as you go along, you can find the completed Chapter 8 code using the link at the end of the Answer Key section.

Section 1: Pandas and Numpy

Python has several libraries for data manipulation and analysis. Two of the most well-known are "Pandas" (Python Data Analysis) and "Numpy" (Numerical Python).

Installing Pandas and NumPy

Before we dive in, go ahead, and create a new folder called "DataAnalysis." Open that folder in VSCode (or the IDE of your choice) and then open a terminal window (CTRL + `). In the terminal window run this command to see if you already have Pandas and NumPy installed:

`pip list`

Scroll through the results and check if Pandas and NumPy are listed. If not, run this command in the terminal to install them:

`pip install pandas`

Under normal circumstances, when you install Pandas, NumPy installs along with it. To be sure, run the "pip list" command to be sure NumPy is also installed. If not, run "pip install numpy" to install it.

Now open a new file in your folder called "panda_data.py". In that file enter this code to import pandas into your module:

import pandas as pd

The "as pd" piece is just an alias you're assigning to the import for ease of reference. For Pandas, the common practice is to use "pd" as the alias. You might be wondering why we're not specifically importing NumPy. This is because Pandas is built on top of NumPy so when you use objects such as DataFrames, any underlying NumPy operations to support them will be handled seamlessly in the background.

To store our data sample, create a subfolder called "DataFiles."

Manipulating Data with Panda

Loading the Data

For this next part, we need some sample data. There is a .csv file for chapter 8 called "BookData.csv." You can download it using the link at the end of the Answer Key section.

Be sure to save it in your "DataFiles" subfolder. You can also use a .csv file of your own if you'd like. Now we need to read the .csv file. So, add this to your code:

```
data = pandas.read_csv('BookData.csv')
```

In your IDE, your code should look something like this:

```
1    import pandas as pd
2
3    data = pd.read_csv('DataFiles/BookData.csv')
```

If, for some reason, you want to skip the first row in your data file, you can modify the above like this:

```
data = pd.read_csv('YourFile.csv', skiprows = 1)
```

If you need to skip more than one consecutive row, you can increase the skiprows number. If you have nonconsecutive rows to skip, you can use line indices to tell the reader what rows to ignore:

```
data = pd.read_csv('YourFile.csv', skiprows =[0,2])
```

This would tell the reader to skip rows 1 and 3. Remember, indexes always start with zero (0), so rows 1 and 3 would equate to 0 and 2.

The Pandas reader is also not limited to reading CSV files. It can read other formats as well, including Excel. Consider this example:

```
1    import pandas as pd
2    # Example with additional parameters
3    excel_data = pd.read_excel('data.xlsx', sheet_name='Sheet1',
4            skiprows=2, usecols=['Column1', 'Column2'])
```

Here, the reader is looking at an Excel file and it is being instructed to read the first sheet, skip the first 2 rows, and only look at columns 1 and 2.'

Exploring the Data

To see what data we have, we'll use a simple print statement:

```
print(data.head())
```

This will print the first few rows of data. If you want a specific number of rows, you can modify it like this:

```
print(data.head(10))
```

To get a summary of statistics in our data, add this line:

```
print(data.describe())
```

Your code should look like this:

```
1    import pandas as pd
2
3    data = pd.read_csv('DataFiles/BookData.csv')
4
5    print(data.head())
6
7    print(data.describe())
```

Save and run this to see the results. You'll probably think, "This is not easy to read." Just hang on! We'll cover data visualization in the next section.

Getting a Better View of CSV Files

CSV files can sometimes be a little difficult to read. If you're using VSCode, you can install the Rainbow CSV extension to make them easier to view. In VSCode, click the "Extensions" icon on the left side of the screen:

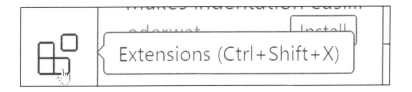

Next, start typing "Rainbow CSV" in the search box. You'll see Rainbow CSV appear in the list.

Click the "Install" button to install it. When you open a CSV file in VSCode, Rainbow CSV will display each column in a different color. There is also an "align columns" feature. Press CTRL+SHIFT+P (Mac users, press the Command button instead of CTRL), and then start typing "Rainbow CSV." Click the "Align CSV Columns" option, and each of the columns will be aligned, making the data more readable. You can remove the alignment by choosing the "Shrink" option.

Listing The Columns in Your Data

Sometimes you just want to see what columns exist in your code to get an idea of what the data covers. To just see what columns exist in your data, add these lines to your code:

```
 9    columns_list = data.columns.tolist()
10    print("Columns in the CSV file:")
11    print(columns_list)
```

The other reason it's good to list your columns is so you can see the columns the way Python sees them. If you installed Rainbow CSV, go ahead, and open the BookData.csv file in VSCode. At the bottom of the screen click the "Align" option and save the CSV file.

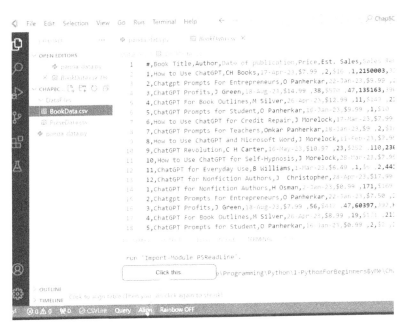

Now go back and run your panda_data.py code and look at the list of column names. Notice the 'Book Title' column for example. The title has a lot of whitespace in it now, and that's how Python sees it. Now, go back to the csv file, click the "Shrink" option at the bottom of the page, and save the file again. Rerun the panda_data.py code and look at the column list. The whitespace is gone, that is how Python sees it now.

Data Selection and Indexing

In our data sample, we have book titles and sales revenue data. Let's say we just want to know what titles are seeing $500 or more in monthly sales. We know that book titles live in a column called 'Book Title' and that sales revenue data lives in a column called 'Sales Rev.' Since we only want to see titles with greater than $500 in monthly sales, we need to filter the data to give back only those rows. So, add this to your code:

```
filtered = data[data['Sales Rev.'] > 500]
```

To cut down on clutter, comment out lines 5, 7, 9-11. Your code should look something like this:

```
panda_data.py > ...
1    import pandas as pd
2
3    data = pd.read_csv('DataFiles/BookData.csv')
4
5    # print(data.head())
6
7    # print(data.describe())
8
9    # columns_list = data.columns.tolist()
10   # print("Columns in the CSV file:")
11   # print(columns_list)
12
13   filtered = data[data['Sales Rev.'] > 500]
```

Line 13: The data type on the "filtered" variable is called a Pandas DataFrame. Within that data frame we are telling our code to only keep records where sales revenue is greater than $500.

Now we need to see the results of that filter *and* the titles of those books. Add these two lines to your code:

```
15   print('Books with sales revenue greater than 500:')
16   print(filtered[['Book Title', 'Sales Rev.']])
```

Line 16: Our "filtered" variable still contains all the columns from our CSV file, but only the records that meet our criteria. However, we do *not* want to see all the columns, just "Book Title" and "Sales Rev.", so we're telling the dataframe to show only those two columns.

Save your code and run it to see the results.

Data Cleansing
When dealing with large sets of data, data integrity issues are not uncommon. These methods in the Pandas library can help with that: *dropna()* and *fillna()*.

Handling of Missing Values	Removes entire rows if any value is missing.	Replaces missing values with a specified value.
Effect on DataFrame Size	May reduce the size of the DataFrame.	Keeps the same number of rows.
Preservation of Data	Loses data in rows with at least one missing value.	Keeps all rows, introducing a default value.
Use Case	Suitable when working with complete cases is critical.	Suitable when replacing missing values with a default value is preferred.
Handling Non-Numeric Data	Works well with both numeric and non-numeric data.	More suitable for numeric data; may need adaptation for non-

numeric data.

(ChatGPT, n.d.)

Dropna()

Let's say that in our data sample, we had rows that were missing data, and we cannot use incomplete rows. By default, dropna() has its axis value set to zero(0) and deletes rows. This line of code would *remove* any rows that had at least one field that was absent of data or null. In Python, absent or null data is referred to as NaN.

```
clean_data = data.dropna()
```

It can be set to delete columns instead if written this way:

```
clean_data = data.dropna(axis=1)
```

Fillna()

This method fills NaN fields with a specified value. This might be useful in situations where you want to keep all the rows and filling the NaN fields will not interfere with how your data is processed.

For example, let's say you have a production signal that is sent to a plant to create widgets. The standard operating procedure is to put a 0 in for locations not receiving any widgets from the plant. However, the person in charge of creating the plant signal accidentally left the quantity field empty for location X. It is now NaN. Location X is not supposed to get any widgets, but the empty field stops the signal from going through to the plant, and this stops all production. Fortunately, the program that handles all of this runs on Python and you just finished reading this paragraph about fillna(). You realize defaulting NaN fields to 0 will not harm anything. In fact, it would save the day. So, you run this line of code to fill the data set:

```
fill_data = data.fillna(0)
```

Now, the quantity field for location X is 0 instead of NaN. The signal goes through, and the plant can continue production. You just saved the company millions! Your manager is elated and says that you're getting a Starbucks gift card in your pay envelope this week. You don't like Starbucks, but you're a team player. So, you smile and say, "Thanks!" Because it's not about the money. It's about the satisfaction that comes from solving a problem and saving the day! (Wink! Wink!)

One More Example

In our book data example, we found one book that was making over $500 in monthly sales. Now let's look at the total revenue for all the books in our sample. Add these two lines to your code, save it, and run it:

```
total_rev = data['Sales Rev.'].sum()

print(f'Total Sales: ${total_rev:.2f}')
```

While having numeric data is nice, for a lot of end users, the information will seem incomplete. "What do the numbers mean? What do they tell us?" As we move onto section 2, we'll broaden our understanding by transitioning from data manipulation to visual storytelling. Data visualization goes beyond numbers. It offers a lens through which we can see patterns, trends, and insights. So, let's apply some simple visualization to our book data analysis.

Section 2: Data Visualization

Let's start with a simple example. We'll create a bar chart. In your IDE, open your "DataAnalysis" folder and create a new file called "bar_chart.py."

Install matplotlib:

Before you can run this code, you need to make sure you have "matplotlib" installed. As we have done earlier, you can check this by running "pip list" in your terminal window to see if it is in your list of installed packages. If you do not have it installed, just run this command:

```
pip install matplotlib
```

Bar Chart Example:

Add this to your code file:

```
1    import pandas as pd
2    import matplotlib.pyplot as plt
```

The import on line 2 is bringing in a specific module from the matplotlib library because we do not need the whole thing.

For our data, we'll use the book data file we used earlier:

```
4    data = pd.read_csv('DataFiles/BookData.csv')
```

Now let's create our DataFrame:

```
6    # Create a DataFrame
7    df = pd.DataFrame(data)
```

The sample data we're using is clean, but it's still good practice to do data cleansing. So, we'll do that here:

```
9    # Filter out rows with NaN values in the 'Est. Sales' column
10   df_filtered = df.dropna(subset=['Est. Sales'])
```

Next, we're going to group our data by format (paperback, hardcover, kindle eBook). The lines shown below are broken up to fit the page. In your code, remove the backslash at the end of the line and make lines 12 and 13 into a single line.

```
12    sales_by_format = df_filtered.groupby \
13    ('Format')['Est. Sales'].sum()
```

This next section will use matplotlib to plot our data:

```
15    # Plotting the data
16    sales_by_format.plot(kind='bar',
17         color=['skyblue', 'lightgreen', 'lightcoral'])
18    plt.title('Estimated Monthly Sales by Format')
19    plt.xlabel('Format')
20    plt.ylabel('Estimated Sales in USD')
21    plt.show()
```

Line 16: The ".plot" piece is a method from Python's pandas library for plotting data from a Panda Series or DataFrame object.

Line 17: Because we know we have only three formats, we can manually choose the colors for the bars in our chart.

Lines 18-20: These determine the title and labels that appear on the chart.

Line 21: This shows us the chart and leaves it open until the chart window is closed.

Go ahead save the code and run it to see the results.

Pie Chart Example:

For this, we only need to change a few lines. So, to save time, make a copy of your bar chart example and rename it "pie_chart.py."

The only change is in the plotting section:

```
14    # Plotting the data as a pie chart
15    plt.pie(sales_by_format, labels=sales_by_format.index,
16        autopct='%1.1f%%', startangle=140,
17        colors=['skyblue', 'lightgreen', 'lightcoral'])
18    plt.title('Estimated Monthly Sales by Format')
19    # Equal aspect ratio ensures that the pie chart is circular.
20    plt.axis('equal')
21    plt.show()
```

Line 15: The "sales_by_format" piece is a Panda Series object. The ".index" represents the formats found in the data set. These become the labels used in the chart.

Line 16: The "autopct" piece displays the percentages that each wedge of the pie represents. If it is set to None, then no percentages display. Putting a numeric format on it shows the percentages. The format used in our example limits the number of decimal places to one.

The "startangle" attribute determines where the first wedge of the pie is placed. You can experiment with this to see how it changes the layout of the pie.

Line 20: The ".axis" attribute determines the scale of the axes in the chart. For our example, setting the axis will have little impact, but for pie charts in general, it's best to set this to "equal" so that the pie remains circular.

Two sides to the same story:
You'll notice that each chart represents the results with a different emphasis. The bar chart does a comparison focused on sales in dollars. The pie chart displays the same data in terms of percentages. Both are important aspects of your data's story.

Both Charts Together
Because our charts give us two parts to the same story, it's natural to want to see them together. So, make a copy of your pie_chart.py code and rename it "both_charts.py."

For this copy, delete everything *below* this line:

```
sales_by_format = df_filtered.groupby('Format')['Est.
Sales'].sum()
```

Now we need to change the plotting section. First, add this:

```
16    # Create subplots (1 row, 2 columns)
17    fig, axs = plt.subplots(1, 2, figsize=(10, 5))
```

Line 17: The "subplots" method of the Matplotlib library creates a new figure and a grid of subplots.

The '1, 2' in our example is creating a table of one row and two columns that will display our grids side by side.

The 'figsize' attribute determines the size of each displayed grid. In our case, each grid will be 10 inches wide by 5 inches tall.

The "subplots" method returns two values: a figure that contains all the elements for the given chart, and an array of Axes (or axs) objects. Think of Axes objects as the elements of the chart structure and the figure as the container that the structure lives in.

Now let's put our charts together:

```
19    # Plotting the data as a bar chart
20    axs[0].bar(sales_by_format.index, sales_by_format,
21        color=['skyblue', 'lightgreen', 'lightcoral'])
22    axs[0].set_title('Estimated Monthly Sales by Format (Bar Chart)')
23    axs[0].set_xlabel('Format')
24    axs[0].set_ylabel('Estimated Sales in USD')
25    axs[0].tick_params(axis='x', rotation=90)
```

Remember, we have two charts, so we have two sets of Axes objects stored in an array. We're using the first one for our bar chart and we'll be using the second one for the pie chart.

To build our second pie chart, add these lines of code:

```
27    # Plotting the data as a pie chart
28    axs[1].pie(sales_by_format, labels=sales_by_format.index, autopct='%1.1f%%',
29        startangle=140, colors=['skyblue', 'lightgreen', 'lightcoral'])
30    axs[1].set_title('Estimated Monthly Sales by Format (Pie Chart)')
31    axs[1].axis('equal')
```

To finish things up, add these last two lines of code, save the file, and run it:

```
33    plt.tight_layout()
34    plt.show()
```

Line 33: This automatically adjusts the layout, so the charts do not overlap.

With both charts side by side, you also have two parts of the same data "story."

Section 3: Making Your Charts Interactive

Adding interactivity to your data visualizations can make your data more engaging and can increase your users' experience. Interactivity can help to make the data seem less abstract.

Install Plotly Express

To get started, we need to install a new module called "Plotly Express." You can do the usual check to see if you already have it, but if you don't, run this command in your terminal window:

```
pip install plotly
```

This may take a few minutes to load. So, be patient. You will also notice that in addition to "plotly," pip will also install a module for "tenacity." The two work together. When I finished installation on my machine, I received a prompt to upgrade pip. I went ahead and did the upgrade. Whether you choose to do the same, is up to you.

Making the Bar Chart Interactive

For this section, we're going to treat the bar chart and pie chart separately. We'll start with the bar chart. Make another copy of your bar_chart.py file and rename the copy "bar_chart_interactive.py."

Changes to the Bar Chart Code

Changes to the imports

Instead of using Matplotlib, we are going to use Plotly. So, change your import statements at the top of your code to this:

```
1    import pandas as pd
2    import plotly.express as px
```

Make a minor change to the group by code

Next, scroll down to the code that handles the group by action and add '.reset_index()' to the end of the line as shown:

```
12    sales_by_format = df_filtered.groupby \
13    ('Format')['Est. Sales'].sum().reset_index()
```

This resets the index on the grouped data so that the chart renders correctly.

Change the plotting code

After making the change to group by code, delete everything below it and replace it with this:

```
15    # Create an interactive bar chart with Plotly Express
16    fig = px.bar(sales_by_format, x='Format', y='Est. Sales',
17            color='Est. Sales',
18            labels={'Est. Sales': 'Estimated Sales in USD'},
19            title='Estimated Monthly' \
20            ' Sales by Format (Interactive)',
21            hover_name='Format')
22
23    # Show the interactive plot
24    # fig.show()
25    fig.write_html('bar_chart.html', auto_open=True)
```

The lines have been wrapped to save space on the page. Format the lines in your code as you see fit. You'll notice that I commented out line 24. If you use line 24 instead of line 25, Plotly will attempt to find an unused port to display its page on your local host. It is not always successful at finding a usable port. Line 25 builds an HTML page, saves it to the current folder, and then displays it. You still get a page with the same interactivity but without the port issues.

Save and run the code.

We are using a very simple data set on purpose to avoid data set issues. So, interactivity with such a small data set may not be necessary, but it does give you proof of concept.

When your page renders, you'll see the bar chart with a place for each of the three formats: Hardcover, Kindle, and Paperback. In our data set, Hardcover will be empty because there are no books in that format for that niche. If you hover your cursor over the other two bars, it will show you the book format and the estimated sales for that format.

If you move your mouse cursor into the upper right corner of the bar chart display, you'll see an icon menu that offers several selection options. Again, our small data set will not do justice to these other features.

Making the Pie Chart Interactive

The process for making the pie chart interactive is similar to what we did for the bar chart.

Change the import lines to this:

```
1    import pandas as pd
2    import plotly.express as px
```

Add '.rest_index() to the group by section:

```
12   sales_by_format = df_filtered.groupby \
13   ('Format')['Est. Sales'].sum().reset_index()
```

Then delete everything below the group by section and replace it with this:

```
14    # Plotting the data as a pie chart
15    plt.pie(sales_by_format, labels=sales_by_format.index,
16        autopct='%1.1f%%', startangle=140,
17        colors=['skyblue', 'lightgreen', 'lightcoral'])
18    plt.title('Estimated Monthly Sales by Format')
19    # Equal aspect ratio ensures that the pie chart is circular.
20    plt.axis('equal')
21    plt.show()
```

The interaction options are fewer with a pie chart and you will find that the interactivity options change depending on the kind of chart you are using.

Further Study

If you want to explore this further, you are encouraged to visit this site:

https://plotly.com/graphing-libraries/

There you'll find information for Plotly as it applies to Python and several other languages and platforms.

Chapter 8 Recap!

In this chapter, we looked at the topic of data analysis and visualization. We used some of the data analysis features available in Python's libraries, specifically Pandas, and we also saw how visualizing data can help communicate its story in a clear and easy-to-grasp way. Additionally, we demonstrated how you can make your charts interactive.

In industry, the trend is toward more and more automation. The mantra is: "If a task needs to be done more than once, it needs to be automated." It's an important consideration because it cuts costs, and improves efficiency. So, in Chapter 9, we'll dive into scripting and automation. See you there!

CHAPTER 9: SCRIPTING & AUTOMATION

Automation is used for a wide range of automation tasks: file manipulation, web and application testing, data scraping, image processing, and more. Not only does it free up valuable IT time, but it also reduces errors and increases efficiency. And automation is not just limited to the corporate world. Every smart appliance from phones, to outlets, to door locks are examples of automation. Forget to lock the doors when you left the house? Just get on your phone and tell your smart locks to lock up. Too cold to start your car in the morning? Use the remote start on your key fob and make the car start itself.

"Implementing IT automation with Python scripts is popular because of the programming language's simplicity, intuitiveness, versatility, support of data structures, and powerful libraries." (Blog, 2023)

In this chapter, we'll cover several hands-on examples to get you familiar with what Python can do when it comes to automation.

Section 1: What is Scripting and Automation?

When we say "scripting and animation" we mean writing scripts in languages like Python to automate tasks. So, scripting is the means and automation is the goal. Scripting is used to handle repetitive tasks. Automation is using technology to perform such tasks with little to no human interaction.

The best way to learn how to do scripting is to get your hands on it. So, the following sections are all hands-on examples.

As always, while I encourage you to write the code as you go, you can find all the code for Chapter 9 using the link at the end of the Answer Key section.

Section 2: File Copier

In your IDE, create a folder called "FileCopier" and make sure your terminal window is working from this folder as well.

For this example, we're going to create a script that copies the files from one folder to another. I chose "copy" instead of "move" just to be safe, but you can change this to move files if that's what you prefer. The user simply provides a source and destination folder, and Python will do the rest.

Setup

In your FileCopier folder create a file called "copy_files.py." In your file include these imports:

```
1    import os
2    import shutil
3    import sys
```

These are all part of the Python Standard Library so there's no need to do

any separate installations for them.

Capture user input

```
5    #Comment out the line below if you want to
6    #prompt the user for a new source directory.
7    sourcedir = input("What folder would you like \
8    me to read from? (Type 'exit' to stop): ")
```

Lines 7 and 8 are wrapped to fit the page. You can combine them into one

line in your code by removing the \ and combine lines 7 and 8 into one.

The While loop

This is the main part of our code. I am breaking this into sections to fit the

page. As you enter it into your code, pay attention to your indentations.

Your IDE should warn you if there are problems.

```
10   while True:
11       #Uncomment the lines 13 and 14 if you want to
12       #prompt the user for a new source directory
13       # sourcedir = input("What folder would you \
14       # like me to read from? (Type 'exit' to stop): ")
15       if sourcedir.lower() == 'exit':
16           break
```

Notice the indentation. Lines 11-16 are all indented underneath the

'while' statement.

Line 10: While loops will run until their conditional statement is True. On this line, we are purposely setting it to True. It will not stop until the user chooses to exit.

Lines 15: This checks to see if the user has opted to exit the application. To ignore case, the user's response is always set to lowercase.

Line 16: This will break out of the 'while' loop and end the program if the user has typed 'exit' in response to the prompt.

These lines prompt the user for a destination directory. They are wrapped to fit the page. In your code combine them into one so you don't have odd spacing in your prompt.

```
18          destinationdir = input("Enter a directory \
19          path to store the output: ")
```

Inner While loop

This 'while' loop is an *inner* loop, meaning it needs to be indented underneath the outer "while' loop and anything inside the inner loop must be indented within it.

This is the opening of the inner while loop.

```
21          while not os.path.exists(destinationdir):
22              print(f"Error: The destination directory '\
23              {destinationdir}' does not exist.")
24              create_dir = input("Do you want to create \
25              the directory? (yes/no): ").lower()
```

Line 21: This checks to see if the directory entered by the user exists.

Lines 22-23: If the directory entered by the user does not exist, these lines let the user know that. *The lines in the screenshot are wrapped.* You will need to remove the \ at the end of line 22 and combine 22 and 23 into one so the prompt displays correctly.

Lines 24-25: These lines ask the user if they want to create the directory because it does not exist. If they answer 'yes,' then a new directory will be created. If they answer 'no,' they will be prompted again for a destination folder. Lines 22-23 and lines 24-25 are wrapped. In your code, convert them into single lines so the prompt displays correctly.

If...elif...else statement
This section is still part of the inner 'while' loop.

```
27          if create_dir == 'yes':
28              os.makedirs(destinationdir)
29              print(f"Directory '{destinationdir}'
30              created.")
31          elif create_dir == 'no':
32              destinationdir = input("Enter a different \
33              directory path: ")
34          else:
35              print("Invalid choice. Please enter \
36              'yes' or 'no'.")
```

Lines 27-30: If the user says 'yes' to creating a new directory, "os.makedirs()" will create a new directory (folder) on the path that was specified by the user and then show them the path. (Lines 28-30 were wrapped to fit the page. Please turn them into a single line in your code.)

Lines 31-33: If the user says 'no' to creating a new directory, the code will prompt the user to enter a different path. Lines 32-33 were wrapped. Convert them into a single line in your code.

Lines 34-36: These lines handle user input errors. Lines 35-36 are wrapped. (You know the drill.)

This line is outside the inner loop but still inside the outer loop.

```
38              lis = os.listdir(sourcedir)
```

The statement "os.listdir" returns a list of file names found in a given directory. Because it is a list, we can iterate through it and perform actions on the individual files in the folder.

These lines are also inside the outer loop:

```
40          for x in lis:
41              print(x)
42              if x == os.path.basename(sys.argv[0]):
43                  continue
44              shutil.copy(os.path.join(sourcedir, x),
45                  destinationdir)
```

Line 41: Shows us what file is being processed.

Lines 41-42: These check to see if the file being processed is the application file itself. If so, it skips it.

Lines 44-45: Python's shell utility is called "shutil" and the copy method performs a simple copy-paste action. The "join" in "os.path.join" joins the file name to the provided directory paths so it knows where the file is coming from and where it's going.

These next lines are the final part of our code and also live inside the outer loop.

```
47          print(f'Files copied from {sourcedir}
48              to {destinationdir}')
49
50          #comment out the line below if you want to
51          # prompt the user for a new source directory
52          sourcedir = 'exit'
```

Lines 47-48: These lines just let the user know the copy action is complete and that files were copied from one folder to the other. The lines are wrapped. So, please make them one line in your code.

Line 52: This simply exits the program.

The way this code works, it will perform the copy action and exit. However, if you follow the instructions in the code comments you can also have the code prompt the user for another folder to copy once it completes.

Copying files is not the only action that Python's shell utility can perform. There are many other such tasks it can do. File management is just one. For example, perhaps your business has a retention policy and for legal reasons, it deletes files greater than 5 years old. You can create a script using shutil methods to delete files that are older than the cut off.

Section 3: File Organizer

Most of us have that folder (or folders) that is the equivalent of a junk drawer. Stuff is in there in no particular order and for no particular reason. This script will go through the contents of a folder and place files in subfolders by type.

Setup

First, create a folder called "FileOrganizer" and make sure your terminal window is pointing here as well. Inside your FileOrganizer folder create a new file called "organizer.py" and then add these imports to it:

```
1     import os
2     import shutil
```

Check if the file exists:

```
4     def organize_files(folder_path):
5         if not os.path.exists(folder_path):
6             print(f"The specified folder path ' \
7                 {folder_path}' does not exist.")
8         return
```

Line 4: This creates the definition for our function.

Line 5: This checks to see if the path entered by the user exists. It returns a Boolean. If it evaluates to False, lines 6 and 7 report this to the user. (Lines 6 and 7 are wrapped. Convert them to a single line in your code.)

Line 8: Note that this lives *inside* the 'if' statement. If the directory does not exist, the 'if' statement returns null and ends the program.

File Type Folder Paths

This section is indented within the definition but outside the preceding 'if' statement. It populates variables for the file type folder paths. You can adjust this as you wish. These do not create the folders. They just hold the paths to them.

```
10        image_folder = os.path.join(folder_path, 'Images')
11        document_folder = os.path.join(folder_path, 'Documents')
12        video_folder = os.path.join(folder_path, 'Videos')
13        gimp_folder = os.path.join(folder_path, 'GIMP')
14        vector_folder = os.path.join(folder_path, 'Vector')
15        other_folder = os.path.join(folder_path, 'Other')
```

As with the file copier we made earlier, the "join" takes the path entered by the user and adds the designated folder onto that path. At this point, these are just strings. The application does not "know" if they exist yet or not.

Create missing folders

Now that our code has the file paths, we can put them in a list and iterate through them with a 'for' loop. If a path does not exist, we will create the corresponding subfolder. This section is indented underneath the definition.

```
18        for folder in [image_folder, document_folder,
19            video_folder, gimp_folder, vector_folder,
20            other_folder]:
21            if not os.path.exists(folder):
22                os.makedirs(folder)
```

Iterate through the files

This is a long for loop. Lines shown in this section are all indented beneath the opening 'for' statement.

```
25        for filename in os.listdir(folder_path):
26            file_path = os.path.join(folder_path, filename)
```

Line 25: The "listdir" function in the "os" library returns a list of everything in the given directory path. As we iterate through each item, we're assigning it to the file_path variable.

These next lines are part of the 'for' loop and should be indented as such.

```
29            if os.path.isdir(file_path):
30                continue
```

If the file path is a directory, we're skipping it. We're only interested in files. The "isdir" function returns True if a path is a directory and not a file. The keyword "continue" instructs the code to go onto the next item in the iteration.

Determine the file type

```
33                    file_type = filename.split('.')[-1].lower()
```

This line splits the file name at the dot between the file name and extension and turns the resulting parts into a list. The [-1] looks for the last item in the list. In this case, that's the extension. The ".lower" at the end of the line converts whatever is found to lowercase. This is so our next section of code can determine what folder to put the file in.

Organize files by type

```
36          if file_type in ['jpg', 'png', 'gif', 'jpeg']:
37              destination_folder = image_folder
38          elif file_type in ['pdf', 'doc', 'docx', 'txt']:
39              destination_folder = document_folder
40          elif file_type in ['mp4', 'avi', 'mkv', 'mov']:
41              destination_folder = video_folder
42          elif file_type in ['xcf']:
43              destination_folder = gimp_folder
44          elif file_type in ['svg']:
45              destination_folder = vector_folder
46          else:
47              destination_folder = other_folder
```

This long 'if' statement is also part of the long 'for' statement and this takes the "file_type" value and determines what the "destination_folder" value should be. For example, on line 36, if the extension is 'jpg', 'png', 'gif', or 'jpeg' the destination_folder value will be the image folder. Any files that do not have a recognized extension will go into the "Other" folder.

Move the files to their folders

This is the last part of the long 'for' statement.

```
50              shutil.move(file_path, os.path.join(
51                  destination_folder, filename))
52              print(f"Moved {filename} to
53                  {destination_folder}")
```

Lines 50-51 and 52-53 are wrapped.

Lines 50-51: These lines use Python's shell utility to move the file to its designated folder depending on the outcome of the previous 'if' statement.

Lines 52-53: These let the user know what file was moved and to where.

This next line is outdented from the 'for' statement but still inside the definition:

```
55          print("File organization completed.")
```

This line just lets the user know the job is complete.

Making the application runnable

This section of code needs to be outdented from the definition. It needs to live outside the definition.

```
57  # Make this a runnable app
58  if __name__ == "__main__":
59      # Get user input for the folder path
60      folder_path = input("Enter the folder path to organize: ")
61
62      # Call the function to organize files
63      organize_files(folder_path)
```

Line 58: This is Python's way of checking if the current script is being run as the main program, or if it is being used as an import. In Python, the special variable '__name__' is set to '__main__' if it is the script that is being run. If a Python script is imported, the '__name__' variable is set to the name of the script that called it. So, the lines below line 58 will only run if the script is run directly. If the script is being imported as a module, only the parts of the method definition will run if requested by the calling script.

Line 60: This prompts the user for a folder to organize.

Line 63: After receiving the user's input, this line calls our method and organizes the files in the selected folder.

Go ahead, save, and run this file from. I recommend making a test folder and putting copies of random files in it. Then run this script against that folder.

Section 4: Bulk Mailer

Sometimes you might have a situation where you need to send emails out to several people in your organization and you need to personalize them. Let's say, for example, each quarter you receive a CSV file with quarterly review scores, and you need to send those results out to each individual. This script will help you parse a CSV file, build the emails, and send them out.

Note: This example uses Gmail. You will need a Google account if you want to follow along with this. Or, you could use this as a template and modify it to use a mail service of your choice.

The CSV file

First, create a folder called "MailerApp". Inside that, create a folder called "DataFiles." For this example, we'll be using a file called "Employees.csv." You can download that file using the link at the end of the Answer Key section.

Save the CSV file in the DataFiles folder. The file contains three fields: name, email, and score. The emails are dummy emails. If you run this script with the dummy emails, you will get a bunch of undeliverable emails sent back to you. I would recommend making at least one of the records have an email address you can send to so you can see your results.

Setup

Now go back to your MailerApp folder and create a new file called "mailer.py." Put these imports in it:

```
1    import csv, smtplib, ssl, os
2    from datetime import date
3    from dotenv import load_dotenv
4    from email.mime.multipart import MIMEMultipart
5    from email.mime.text import MIMEText
```

Most of these are part of the Python standard library, but you will probably need to install 'python-dotenv.' If you're not sure, just run 'pip list' in your terminal window to see if python-dotenv is installed. If it isn't, run this command:

```
pip install python-dotenv
```

Create a .env file

In your MailerApp folder, create a ".env" file. This file will contain the app password you'll need to run the mailer app. We'll be using Gmail as our email program and an app password is required. Your personal Gmail password will not work.

Load_dotenv()

Add this line to your code.

```
7    load_dotenv()
```

This line is needed so that our code can access the .env file. Go ahead and open your .env file and make this entry:

```
email=YOUR_EMAIL_ADDRESS
```

Change YOUR_EMAIL_ADDRESS to your actual email without quotes and save the file. The .env file is a key-value file. We use the key to get to the value without exposing it in our code. If you plan to commit this code to a GitHub repo, also create a .gitignore file and add .env to that file so when you commit your code to the online repo, that information remains hidden.

Date and Sender Email Values

Now add these lines to your code.

```
9     today = date.today().strftime('%B %d, %Y')
10    from_address = os.getenv("email")
```

Line 9: This gets the current date and formats it. The parameters in the "strftime" method evaluate to month, date, and year.

Example: December 28, 2023

Line 10: This is accessing the "email" key in the .env file and populates the "from_address" variable with the email address we assigned to it.

Getting Your App Password

To get the code to work with Gmail, you'll need an app password. You can attempt to get one here:

https://myaccount.google.com/apppasswords

If the link does not work, follow these steps:

1. Open Google Chrome.

2. Go to your account at https://myaccount.google.com/.(If you do not have an account, you will need to open one. It's free.)

3. Click "Security" on the side panel.

4. In the "How you sign into Google" section, click on "2-Step Verification."

5. Scroll down to the bottom of the page and click on "App passwords."

6. You'll see an entry field where you need to enter a name for your app. It can be anything you want.

7. Click "create" and copy the password you are shown.

8. Open your .env file.

9. Create a new line in that file and enter this:

pwd=THE_APP_PASSWORD_YOU_JUST_GOT

The line should have "pwd=" followed by your app password with no quotes.

Now add these lines to your code:

```
13    password = os.getenv("pwd")
14    context = ssl.create_default_context()
```

Line 13: This populates the "password" variable with the password from your .env file.

Line 14: This creates a default SSL (secure socket layer) context using the SSL module in Python.

The "With" Statements

The rest of this script involves two "with" statements: one out and one inner. This is the start of the opening "with" statement:

```
16    with smtplib.SMTP_SSL('smtp.gmail.com', 465,
17            context=context) as server:
18        server.login(from_address, password)
```

Lines 16-17: These lines open a secure connection with Gmail's SMTP (Simple Mail Transfer Protocol).

"'smtp.gmail.com', 465" represents the hostname and port number needed to make secure connections to Gmail's SMTP server.

Lines 16 and 17 are wrapped and you can convert these to a single line if you want.

Line 18: This performs the login using your provided email and app password.

These next lines of code need to be indented beneath the outer "with" statement:

```
20          with open(r'DataFiles\Employees.csv') as file:
21              reader = csv.reader(file)
22              next(reader)
```

This is our *inner* "with" statement. "With" statements make it easier to manage resources such as files and network connections and are common to many programming languages.

Line 20: This opens our CSV for processing. The "r" in the statement lets us use the raw string path without having to "escape" the backslash in the file path with double backslashes: "\\".

Line 21: This uses the CSV module in Python to open a CSV reader. The reader is just one of several features available in Python's csv module.

Line 22: Our csv has a header row. This line tells the reader to skip to the next row so we do not process the header row.

These next lines need to be indented inside the inner "with" at the same level as lines 21 and 22:

```
24      for row in reader:
25          name = row[0]
26          email = row[1]
27          score = row[2]
```

Lines 24-27: This is just a simple "for loop" that iterates through each field in the row to retrieve the data. Because rows are indexed, and indexes always start with 0, we can access each field just by using its index starting with index 0.

These next lines need to be indented inside the "for loop" at the same level as lines 25-27.

```
29          subject = "Your evaluation"
30          body = f"""Hi, {name}, the date of your Q1 evaluation
31          was {today}. Your post-evaluation score is: {score}.
32          You'll receive a separate confidential email giving
33          you a detailed breakdown of your results."""
```

These populate what will become your email message. The "body" variable is a formatted string and has been wrapped to fit the page. Please make this a single line in your code or it will not format correctly in your email.

These next lines of code also need to be indented inside the "for loop" at the same level as the lines above them:

```
35          message = MIMEMultipart()
36          message['From'] = from_address
37          message['To'] = email
38          message['Subject'] = subject
39          message.attach(MIMEText(body, 'plain'))
40          print(f"Attempting to send email to {name} at {email}.")
41          #  print(f"{message.as_string}") # For debugging
42
43          # Send the email
44          server.sendmail(from_address, email,
45          message.as_string().encode('utf-8'))
```

Lines 35-41: This uses parts of Python's email module to create a multipart email to make sure each section goes into the correct field in the email and preps the message as plain text. Lin 41 can be commented out for debugging purposes to see what the message will look like.

Lines 44-45: These lines are wrapped and can be converted into one line if you want. If you're debugging, you can comment these out until you're satisfied with the message.

Running the code

First, be sure your terminal window is in your MailerApp window. Also, check to make sure at least one of the recipients in the Employees.csv has an email address you can access. Then, if you're using VSCode, click the run button, or use whatever run option your IDE uses.

Chapter 9 Recap!

In this chapter, we discovered what scripting and automation are, why it's useful, and why Python with its combination of simplicity and power is a popular choice for this kind of task. To demonstrate some of what Python can do in this arena, we went over several hands-on scripting examples. The examples given in this chapter only scratch the surface when it comes to scripting and automation, but they give you a good exposure to Python's potential. We have one more concept to cover: interacting with databases. In Chapter 10 we are going to look at database basics and Python integration. See you there!

CHAPTER 10: DATABASE BASICS & PYTHON INTEGRATION

N this final chapter, we'll delve into connecting Python to databases and mastering CRUD operations (Create, Read, Update, Delete). Whether you're aspiring to build dynamic web applications, manage large datasets, or enhance your scripting capabilities, working with databases is a vital programming skill. Let's start with the basics.

Section 1: Introduction to Databases

What is a Database

Put simply, a database is a collection of related data organized in a way that is quickly accessible, and usually stored on a computer or similar device.

Types of Databases: Relational and NoSQL

Relational Databases:

Rather than try to paraphrase, here is a direct quote from Oracle.com:

"A [relational] database is an organized collection of structured information, or data.... A database is usually controlled by a database management system (DBMS). Together, the data and the DBMS, along with the applications that are associated with them, are referred to as a database system, often shortened to just database." (*What Is a Database?*, n.d.)

In relational databases, data is modeled in tables that are arranged in columns and rows. Most use structured query language (SQL) for querying their data.

Three popular relational database systems (RDBS) are SQLite, MySQL, and PostgreSQL.

- SQLite is a serverless, lightweight, and self-contained DB that is best suited for small to medium-sized projects and applications where simple and minimal configuration is key. SQLite is great for local storage applications, mobile apps, and desktop software.

- MySQL is an open-source relational database management system (RDBMS) that is good for large-scale operations and websites. It is known for its scalability, uses a client-server architecture, and allows for multiple-user access. You typically see this kind of DB in content management systems (CMS), web applications, and large-scale corporate environments.

- PostgreSQL, like the other two, is also open source. It is known for its extensibility, scalability, and SQL compliance, and is well-suited to large-scale applications. It is often used for projects requiring advanced features such as data warehousing and large-scale information systems.

NoSQL Databases:

These are DBs that do not follow the structured database model. Two popular NoSQL database systems include MongoDB and Redis.

- MongoDB is document-oriented and stores data in BSON documents, which are similar to JSON documents. (Our weather app uses JSON documents for its data.) Because it is schema-less, it is well-suited to data environments that are more dynamic and less structured. You would most likely find this kind of DB in use on social media platforms and real-time analytics tools.

- Redis uses an in-memory key-value model. It is often used as a caching mechanism for fast data retrieval. It's well-suited for applications requiring real-time information such as gaming or messaging apps. While that description may give the impression that its memory is volatile (meaning what it stores immediately vanishes when the app is done), by default, it is configured to use "snapshotting" and "append-only file" (AOF) for long-term storage to disc.

Five Things to Consider When Selecting a Database for Your Python Application:

As you can tell from the previous discussion, there is no one answer to the question: "What is *the* best database to use with Python?" The best answer to that is, "It depends." Here are five things to consider:

One: Data Structure and Complexity

If you know your data will have (or need) well-defined structures and relationships, a relational database system makes the most sense. If your data is more fluid and prone to change, a NoSQL database is the better choice.

Two: Scalability Requirements

If you anticipate your project will experience significant growth in the future, consider using a DBS that can scale with your demand. Using a DB that is less scalable and simpler to use may seem like a good idea at first, but having to scramble to keep up with growth and migrate to a more robust system can prove problematic.

Three: Community and Support

What sort of community and support is behind the DB system you're considering? Good community support means access to resources, know-how, and quicker bug fixes. You want your project married to a stable database system, not the crazy cat lady. (Apologies to any non-crazy cat ladies.)

Four: Project Size and Complexity

Size and complexity do not necessarily go hand in hand. You might have a large project that only needs a simple database. Larger, more complex projects might need the advanced capabilities of something like PostgreSQL. Others may not.

Five: Integration with Python

Make sure that the database you choose to work with Python has a Python driver that is well-supported. There may be situations where you're asked to work with an established DB and changing DBs is out of the question. While you might be able to make a tailor-made connection between Python and that DB, keep in mind that you will have to be able to maintain that connection over time. That would include keeping it working through upgrades in both Python and the given DB. If the DB cannot be changed, you may need to consider a solution other than Python. Because, ultimately, your goal is to have your application and your DB work together seamlessly.

Section 2: Basic SQL CRUD Operations

CRUD stands for "Create, Read, Update, and Delete." These are standard operations in SQL. Technically, "create" is for INSERT statements, and "read" is for SELECT statements, but that would spell "ISUD" and who would remember that?

CRUD operations apply to both RDMS (relational database management system) and NoSQL databases. However, NoSQL CRUD commands vary from system to system. Some NoSQL DBs use a query language similar to SQL, while others handle them with built-in functions. The examples shown below are for RDBMS systems (CrowdStrike, 2023).

Create (Insert):

```
INSERT INTO <table name> VALUES (field value 1, field
value, 2…)
```

Read (Select):

```
SELECT field 1, field 2, …FROM <table name> [WHERE
<condition>]
```

The "WHERE" clause is optional and is used to apply search conditions to pull a specific set of records.

Update:

```
UPDATE <table name> SET field1=value1, field2=value2,…
[WHERE <condition>]
```

The "WHERE" clause here is technically optional but usually a good idea so that you don't accidentally update more records than you planned. Also, it's good practice to run a SELECT statement first and then turn it into an UPDATE statement to be sure you're only affecting the records you mean to affect.

Delete:

```
DELETE FROM <table name> [WHERE <condition>]
```

As with the UPDATE statement, the "WHERE" clause is optional but usually a good idea. It's also good to run a SELECT query first before turning it into a DELETE query just to be sure you don't accidentally delete more than you planned. Does it happen? Yes. I know of a situation where a terabyte of information was deleted by an incorrect deletion action. You don't want to be that guy. That guy didn't want to be that guy.

Section 3: Database Example

This section walks you through connecting Python to a database and performing simple CRUD actions. As always, I encourage you to write the code as you read through the steps. However, if you prefer, you can download the completed code using the link at the end of the Answer Key section.

To Run This Code

If you want to run this code, you will need to install MySQL Server on your machine. If you are not comfortable with doing that, you can still follow along through the code and learn how to connect and interact with a DB in Python. You will just not be able to perform the database actions.

Installing MySQL Server

Please read all these steps BEFORE downloading or installing anything so you know what is involved.

For Windows

Download the MySQL Server installer from here:

https://dev.mysql.com/downloads/installer/

As of this writing, when you get to the installer page, there are two "flavors." I went with the smaller one. After clicking that link, you'll be prompted to open a free Oracle account. You *don't have to open an account.* You can click the link that says: "No thanks, just start my download" instead.

After downloading the installer, open it and follow the prompts.

Installing MySQL Server for Other Operating Systems

If you want to install MySQL Server for a different OS, please go to this link and follow the instructions there:

https://dev.mysql.com/doc/refman/5.7/en/installing.html

For All Systems

Choosing a MySQL Server Setup Type

To save space on my machine, I chose the "Server only" option. You can choose the full setup if you prefer. From there, continue following the prompts.

Type and Networking

For "Config Type" I chose "Development Computer." I left everything else at the default settings.

Authentication Method

I opted for the recommended setting.

Accounts and Roles

Enter a password and save it somewhere!

Click the "Add User" button and create a user for yourself with the DB Admin role. Choose a user name for yourself. Leave the "Host" and "<All Hosts (%)>" as is. Enter your user credentials and remember those as well! I used the same for both screens. Probably not the best idea, but easy to remember.

Click "Next."

Windows Service

Leave these at their defaults, unless you have a reason not to, and click "Next."

Server File Permissions

Leave the settings as is, unless you have a reason not to, and click "Next."

Apply Configuration

Click "Execute." After the execution completes, click "Finish." Follow the prompts to complete the installation. You'll be prompted to copy the log to the clipboard. You can save it if you want for later reference.

Connecting Python to a MySQL DB

Create a DB in MySQL

Open the MySQL Command-Line Client and run this command:

```
Create database Quotes;
```

You can make your DB name something else if you prefer, but in this example, we'll be creating a small DB of quotes.

Building the Python Script

Create a Folder:

In your IDE, create a folder called to contain the DB example. I called mine "PyDbSample."

Create Your Files:

In that folder, create the following files:

- .env
- .gitignore
- create.py
- delete.py
- my_sql_db.py
- read.py
- show_records.py
- update.py

I know this is a lot of files but the goal is to modularize our code, keep clutter to a minimum in our main file, and keep each CRUD action in a separate file for ease of reference.

The "Dot" Files

The .env file is for storing the username and password you created earlier when you installed MySQL Server. This way we can access that information in our code without exposing it.

In the .env file, create a line for user and another for password. When you're done, your file should look something like this:

user=YourUsername

password=YourPassword

Change "YourUsername" to your username without quotes and "YourPassword" to your password without quotes.

In the ".gitignore" file enter ".env" in it without the quotes and save it. This is in case you decide to deploy your code to GitHub.

The Other Files

The other files will come into play and make more sense as we develop our code.

Install the Necessary Modules

Two modules need to be installed for this example. Install the mysql-connector with this command.

```
pip install mysql-connector-python
```

And because we need to access the .env file for environment variables, also install python-dotenv with this command:

```
pip install python-dotenv
```

Add Your Imports

In your "my_sdl_db.py" file, add these lines:

```
1    from dotenv import load_dotenv
2    import mysql.connector, os
3    from mysql.connector import Error
```

Line 1 should look familiar. It allows you to access your .env file.

Lines 2 uses the connector module and will allow us to access and manipulate our database. It is also importing the os module so we can access the username and password from the .env file.

Line 3 is pulling in the Error class so our code can handle MySQL errors more efficiently.

Building the Supporting Files

Before we continue with our main file, we're going to fill in the other support Python script files we created. We'll do the first four in CRUD order.

The Create Script

Open your create.py file and enter these lines of code:

```
1    # Creates records using INSERT query
2
3    def create_record(cursor, source, saying, category):
4        insert_query = "INSERT INTO \
5            Sayings(Source, Saying, Category) \
6            VALUES (%s, %s, %s)"
7        values = (source, saying, category)
8
9        cursor.execute(insert_query, values)
10
```

In your code, it would be better to remove the backslashes (\) at the end of lines 4 and 5 and to turn lines 4-6 into a single line. It's wrapped here to fit the page.

Purpose: As stated in the comment, this function creates a creates a record using an INSERT query.

KEYWORDS / PHRASES:

- INSERT INTO is the command that inserts new records into a database table. In the INSERT clause, you name the fields (columns) you are affecting. Columns that are not required do not have to be named in the INSERT.

- The VALUES clause represents the values you are putting into the record and must match the number, data type, and position of the columns named in the insert clause. So, for example, if I have a table with columns A, B, C, and D where A is a number column and the rest are text columns, and my INSERT clause is "INSERT INTO MyTable (A, B, C, D)" then my VALUES need to be arranged as number, text, text, text. If my INSERT clause is "INSERT INTO MyTable(B,A,C,D) then my VALUES need to be arranged as text, number, text, text.

Line 3: This opens the definition and takes four parameters:

- A **cursor** is an object that allows you to interact with a database and use queries to fetch records.

- **Source**, **saying**, and **category** are parameters for the SQL statement.

Lines 4-6: These lines populate the "insert_query" variable with the INSERT statement. In our function, instead of values, we have placeholders: %s, %s, %s. At runtime, these are replaced by the values passed to the function.

Line 7: This populates the "values" variable with the values passed to the function.

Line 8: This uses the cursor object to execute the query.

The Read Script
Now open the read.py file and enter these lines of code:

```
1    # Reads records from a table using SELECT query.
2
3    def read_records(cursor, condition=None):
4        if condition == None:
5            select_query = f"SELECT * FROM Sayings"
6        else:
7            select_query = f"SELECT * \
8            FROM Sayings WHERE {condition}"
9
10       cursor.execute(select_query)
11
12       return cursor.fetchall()
```

Purpose: This runs a SELECT query that pulls records from a DB table.

Keywords / Phrases:

- The SELECT keyword names the columns (fields) you want returned by the SELECT statement. Using the wildcard symbol '*' returns all the fields in the row. You can also opt to name specific fields (columns) in the row. So, if a row has fields A, B, C, D, and you only want fields A and D, you could write SELECT, A, D....

- The FROM keyword identifies the table(s) from which you want to pull records.
- The WHERE clause is optional. With a WHERE clause, you can set conditions to limit which rows you pull into your data set. (SELECT queries do NOT alter data. They only SHOW data based on the query.)

Line 3: This opens the definition, and it takes two variables:

- We've already discussed the **cursor** object.
- The **condition** is defaulted to None, meaning that a condition does not need to be passed in. This would be the case if you wanted all the records in the table returned.

Lines 4-8: This "if...else" statement handles both a plain SELECT statement and one with a condition.

Line 10: As with our create example, the cursor object is used to run the SELECT query.

Line 12: This returns the results of the "fetchall()" method which returns a list of all the rows from a result set.

The Update Script

Now open the update.py file and enter these lines of code:

```
1    # Updates records using an UPDATE query.
2
3    def update_record(cursor, new_values, condition):
4        update_query = f"UPDATE Sayings SET \
5            {new_values} WHERE {condition}"
6
7        cursor.execute(update_query)
```

Purpose: Updates records in a table using an update query. An update can update an entire record or only a part of one.

Keywords / Phrases:

- UPDATE identifies the table whose records are being updated.
- SET provides the update values.
- The WHERE clause limits the records being updated to a specific set based on a condition.

Line 3: This opens the definition and takes three variables:

- The **cursor** variable has already been discussed.
- The **new_values** are the values that will replace the current values in the record.
- The **condition** value affects what records will be updated and it is *not* set to a default, meaning all three variables in this function are required.

Lines 4-5: These populate the "update_query" variable with our update query. The lines can be combined into one in your code if you want.

Line 7: As in our other files, this uses the cursor object to execute the query.

The Delete Script

Now open the delete.py file and enter these lines of code:

```
1    # Deletes records using a DELETE query.
2
3    def delete_records(cursor, condition=None):
4        if (condition == None):
5            delete_query = f"DELETE FROM Sayings"
6        else:
7            delete_query = f"DELETE FROM Sayings\
8                WHERE {condition}"
9
10       cursor.execute(delete_query)
11
12       return cursor.rowcount
```

Purpose: Delete records with a DELETE query.

Keywords / Phrases:

- DELETE FROM does not need to include anything else except the table from which you want to delete records. If used without a condition, DELETE will delete all records from a table. If you have an autoincrement field like our Sayings table does, and add records after having deleted them all, the autonumbering will pick up where it left off. It will not go back to 1.

- A WHERE clause can be used to limit the records being deleted. If you delete a record and insert a new one in a table with an autoincrementing ID field, the numbering will continue and there will be a gap in the sequence where records have been deleted. For example, if you have 10 records in your table and you delete record 5 and then create a new record, the new record will get an ID of 11, not 5.

Line 3: Opens the definition and takes two parameters:

- The **cursor** object has already been discussed.

- The **condition** parameter is defaulted to None, so this function can be called without a condition in which case all the records from the table would be deleted.

Lines 4-8: These lines handle the DELETE request. The "if" does a full delete and the "else" handles deletes based on a condition.

Line 10: Uses the cursor object to run the DELETE query.

Line 12: This returns the number of records that were deleted.

The Show Records Script

We will use this function to show the user different record sets as the main script progresses. Open your show_records.py file and add these lines of code:

```
1    def display_records(records, description="Records:"):
2        print(description + "\n")
3        for row in records:
4            print("ID = ", row[0])
5            print("Source = ", row[1])
6            print("Saying = ", row[2])
7            print("Category = ", row[3])
8            print("\n")
```

Line 1: This opens the definition and takes two parameters:

- The RECORDS parameter is a list of records from a dataset.

- The DESCRIPTION parameter is a string that is defaulted to just say "Records" if no other string is passed in.

Line 2: Prints the description and adds a line break. (That's what the "\n" is doing.)

Lines 3-7: This iterates the list of records. For each row, it displays the contents in each field within the row. It accesses the fields using the index.

Line 8: This just prints a line break.

Back to the Main Script

Now that we have our support files written, let's import them into the my_sql_db.py file. At the top of your code, add these imports:

```
1    from dotenv import load_dotenv
2    import mysql.connector, os
3    from mysql.connector import Error
4    from create import create_record
5    from read import read_records
6    from update import update_record
7    from delete import delete_records
8    from show_records import display_records
```

You should already have lines 1-3. You'll need to add lines 4-8.

About the Import Syntax:

Lines 4-8 have the same syntax as line 1. They are written this way to import a specific function from the module. This is so it's easier to refer to the function within our main module. For example, if we just did "import create," we'd still have access to the module and its single function but in our main module we'd have to call create's function by its fully-qualified name: "create.create_record()." That would be like having a friend who insisted that you call them by their full name and their name was "John Jacob Jingleheimerschmidt." By using the "from...import" syntax we only need to use the function name because our main module would see the function as part of its own code.

Username and Password

To log into our DB we need to get the username and password from our .env file. Add these lines of code:

```
10    load_dotenv()
11
12    username = os.getenv("user")
13    pwd = os.getenv("password")
```

Create the 'Sayings' Table

When we created the "Quotes" DB we created an empty DB. To create a table, we need to run a CREATE TABLE query. So, let's create a variable and assign the query to it.

```
15    # Create table query
16    table_qry = """CREATE TABLE IF NOT EXISTS Sayings(
17                  Id INT PRIMARY KEY AUTO_INCREMENT,
18                  Source VARCHAR(250) NOT NULL,
19                  Saying VARCHAR(1400) NOT NULL,
20                  Category VARCHAR(250))
21                      """
22
```

The query we're using uses "CREATE TABLE IF NOT EXISTS." This takes advantage of MySQL's ability to handle conditions. So, our code doesn't have to check if the table exists. MySQL will do that for us and only create our table if it is not already there.

On **line 17**, we're creating a primary key that uses integers. We are also setting it to autoincrement. This way, we don't have to create a unique ID for each record. That also means that when we create records, we don't have to remember to include an ID.

Lines 18-20 create the rest of our columns (fields). In a DB, each row consists of fields which can also be referred to as columns. When columns are created the column name, data type, and size are declared.

Try...Except...Finally Block

In this section, we're going to use a "try...except...finally" block to make the connection to our DB. (We'll call it a "TEF block" for short.) The "try" section will attempt to make the connection to our DB. The "except" section will display a message if errors are encountered. The "finally" section runs whether an error occurs or not.

The Try Block:

```
23   # Establish connection and perform actions
24   try:
25       connection = mysql.connector.connect(host='localhost',
26                                      database='Quotes',
27                                      user=username,
28                                      password=pwd)
29
```

Lines 24-28 open the connection to our "Quotes" database. And because we are using a .env file for our username and password, they are not exposed in our code.

The "if" block we are creating below is all indented *inside* the "try" block and makes up the remainder of the "try" block. It is broken up into several parts.

The If Block – Display Connection Info:

```
30       if connection.is_connected():
31           db_Info = connection.get_server_info()
32           print("Connected to MySQL Server version ", db_Info)
33           cursor = connection.cursor()
34           cursor.execute("select database();")
35           record = cursor.fetchone()
36           print("You're connected to database: ", record)
```

This section first checks to see if the connection is open, and if it is it reports the MySQL server version and the name of the database you're connected to.

The If Block – Drop Table:
This next section continues our if statement. This section of code came because of my development efforts to get this to work just right. Rather than delete records for each new run, I opted to wipe the table out and start over. The block is self-explanatory.

```
38          # Drop old table if it exists
39          cursor.execute("DROP TABLE IF EXISTS Sayings")
40          connection.commit()
41          print("'Sayings' table dropped!")
```

As with the query the table query back on like 16, this query also takes advantage of MySQL's ability to handle conditions. The DROP TABLE action only occurs if the table already exists. Just so you're aware, some database actions can be rolled back. Dropping a table cannot be. Be mindful of that when you're working on a database that deals with vital information.

The If Block – Create Table
Before we can begin adding data and manipulating it, we need to create a table.

```
43          # Create fresh table
44          cursor.execute(table_qry)
45          connection.commit()
46          print("'Sayings' table created!")
```

This code uses the "table"qry" variable we created earlier to create the "Sayings" table where we'll store our quotes.

The "connection.commit()" statements in our DROP TABLE and CREATE TABLE sections are more a formality than a necessity. Both are READ ONLY actions that cannot be undone. So, they are technically committed once they are performed.

Adding Our CRUD Functions

These are still part of the "if" statement. What we are including here are the modules we created earlier.

Creating Records for Our Quotes

We're going to use our "create" module to add our six quotes to the DB:

```
48          # Insert (create) record(s).
49          create_record(cursor,"Albert Einstein",
50              "There are only two ways to live your life. \n"\
51                  "One is as though nothing is a miracle. \n"\
52                  "The other is as though everything is a miracle.",
53                  "inspirational, life, miracles")
54
55          create_record(cursor, "Abraham Lincoln",
56              "You can't believe everything you hear on the Internet.",
57                  "inspirational, wisdom, truth")
```

```
59      create_record(cursor, "Thomas Edison",
60          "I have not failed. I've just found 10,000 ways that won't work.",
61              "inspirational, failure, paraphrased")
62
63      create_record(cursor, "Steve Martin",
64          "A day without sunshine is like, you know, night.",
65              "humor, obvious")
```

```
67          create_record(cursor, "C. S. Lewis",
68              "You can never get a cup of tea large enough or a \
69                  book long enough to suit me.",
70                  "books, reading, tea")
71
72          create_record(cursor, "Proverbs 3:13",
73              "Happy is the man that findeth wisdom, and the man \
74                  that getteth understanding.",
75              "Bible, Scripture, truth, wisdom")
```

Reading Our New Records

Now that we've entered our quotes, we're going to read them with our "read" module.

```
77          # Read (select) records
78          records = read_records(cursor)
79          display_records(records,"Selected records:")
```

Line 78 calls our read_records method and passes in the cursor object. The method then returns a list that we're using to populate our "records" variable. Note that "read_records" can take *two* arguments but we're only sending in one because the second parameter in our method, "condition," is set to None by default.

Line 79 calls the "display_records" method and will display all the records we've entered.

Updating A Record

One of our records is not completely accurate. Abraham Lincoln did not say, "You can't believe everything you hear on the Internet." So, let's put in something he *did* say.

First, we're going to display the original quote.

```
81          # BEFORE update:
82          records = read_records(cursor, "Source like '%Lincoln%'")
83          display_records(records, "Pre-change")
```

In this call to the "read_records" method, we're sending in a condition:

$$\text{"Source like '\%Lincoln\%'"}$$

The LIKE keyword will look for data that contains a particular element. In our case, we want to look for an entry in the "Source" column that contains the word "Lincoln." In SQL, one of the wildcard characters is the "%" symbol. This means "include any number of characters." Our condition has "'%Lincoln%'" which means "look for a string with any number of characters before "Lincoln" and any number of characters after "Lincoln." Notice that the whole conditional statement is surrounded by single quotes. If the condition is not wrapped like that, SQL will throw an error.

When this runs, "display_records" will show only one record because only one record in our "Sayings" table has a source that contains the word "Lincoln."

Next, we want to update that record with a proper quote.

```
85        update_record(cursor,
86            new_values="Saying = 'Let us diligently apply the means, \n"\
87                "never doubting that a just God, in His own good time, \n"\
88                "will give us the rightful result.'",
89            condition="Source LIKE '%Lincoln%'")
```

In this call to "update_record," I have written out the parameters and given them values (except for cursor which does not need one). This is just for clarity. As long as each parameter is separated by a comma, the call will work. You do not have to write out the parameter names like I did.

To see if the update was successful, we'll do another call to "display_records":

```
91        # AFTER update:
92        records = read_records(cursor, "Source like '%Lincoln%'")
93        display_records(records, "Post-change")
```

When this code runs, you'll see the updated information in the record. Also, note that the ID on the record will be unchanged because this is not a new record; it's an updated one.

Deleting a Record
Now let's call our "delete_records" method to delete a record:

```
95          # Delete records
96          deletions = delete_records(cursor, "Source = 'Steve Martin'")
97          print(f"{deletions} records deleted.\n")
98
99          records = read_records(cursor)
100         display_records(records, "Remaining records:")
101
102         connection.commit()
```

On **Line 96** we are calling "delete_records" with a condition. If we don't, *all* our records will be deleted. Our condition only deletes records where "Source = 'Steve Martin'". Notice the single quotes around 'Steve Martin'. Also, note that this time we did an "equals" instead of a LIKE. So, this condition is going to look for a string that exactly matches the string "Steve Martin." (Nothing against him, by the way.)

Lines **99-100** display the records after the deletion and you will notice in the output that there is a break in the ID sequence because a record was deleted.

Line 102 runs a "commit" statement that commits all our record changes to the table.

This is the end of our "if" block.

Why is a "commit" statement necessary?

Even though we can see the changes we made to the records in our DB, they are not made permanent without executing the "commit" statement. Instead, our changes are held in a temporary space outside the DB. This is so you can roll back your transactions using the SQL "rollback" command if you realize a mistake has been made. If you have multiple users logged onto a database and you forget to commit your transactions, the other users will not see your changes because until you commit them, your changes are only visible to you in your current session.

The Except Block:

This block lives at the same indentation level as our "try" block so it's on the left of our "if" section. It will capture any SQL errors in our code at runtime and display a message in the terminal explaining what it is.

```
104     except Error as e:
105         print("Error while connecting to MySQL", e)
```

On **line 104,** the "Error" class comes from the import we did on line 3 and focuses only on MySQL errors. So, if one of our SQL commands has an error, that "Error" class will capture it and explain the problem in the terminal window. That said, understand that any errors it shows will be within the context of SQL command, not our Python code.

Here's an example error:

Error while connecting to MySQL 1064 (42000): You have an error in your SQL syntax; check the manual that corresponds to your MySQL server version for the right syntax to use near 'us diligently apply the means,

never doubting that a just God, in His own good ' at line 1

This error is from line 86 in my Python code, but the error says it is at line 1. That's because it is only looking at my SQL code and it consists of only one line. (I removed a single quotation mark from the SQL command to trigger the error.) To help you track the error, it gives you a hint stating that the error is near 'us diligently apply the means, never doubting that a just God, in His own good '. With that, you can track where that statement is in your code and study the SQL command.

Hint: If you take the errant SQL command and put it in Notepad++, you can set Notepad++ to read it as SQL and the color coding can help you see the error.

Optionally, you could take that section of Python code and dump it into ChatGPT like this:

"What is wrong with this Python code? It is throwing a SQL error: [DUMP YOUR CODE HERE]" where [DUMP YOUR CODE HERE] is replaced by your actual code. By phrasing it that way, you're telling ChatGPT that it is analyzing Python code and that the code is trying to use an SQL command.

Time to Run the Code!

If you installed MySQL server, can run this code. If you did not unwrap the lines I wrapped to fit the page, you might see some oddly formatted output due to extra whitespace. You might also run into syntax errors because of the wrapping. So, please check for that. If nothing else, you can download the completed code using the link at the end of the Answer Key section and use that for comparison.

Chapter 10 Recap!

Congratulations! You made it through to the end of Chapter 10! Here's what we covered in this chapter:

- How to connect Python to a database.

- Different kinds of databases and how to determine what DBMS to use for different projects.

- CRUD: Create, Read, Update, and Delete.

- Import syntax and why it is necessary to import specific functions from a module.

- AND we built a sample DB and did some database manipulation.

Great work! Pat yourself on the back for staying with it. Now it's time to wrap things up.

CONCLUSION

When the Apostle John ended his gospel on the Lord Jesus Christ, he wrote: "And there are also many other things which Jesus did, the which, if they should be written every one, I suppose that even the world itself could not contain the books that should be written. Amen." (John 21:25)

I am by no means implying that the book you're reading right now is a gospel – *not at all!*

I quote that verse because writing anything that strives to lay down foundational principles is not as simple as it seems on the surface. What do you include? What do you exclude? When do you decide, "OK. Let's stop here." Those are not easy choices to make and if it seems we've only scratched the surface, you're right. For Python and any other coding language, there is always more to learn and more to discover than what you can fit in a book, explain in a video, or teach in a course. But a good education doesn't teach you *everything*. Instead, it gives you a solid foundation and teaches you how to learn the next thing. I hope that I accomplished that for you in this book. I encourage you to keep on learning!

So, what did we cover in the span of this book on Python programming for beginners?

We covered Python essentials such as what is Python and why to use it? We went over how to set up your IDE (and what an IDE is). We talked about data types in Python, and what you'll find as you continue learning is that much of what we covered about Python applies to other languages too. So, I encourage you to expand your horizons and become "multilingual" in programming languages.

What else did we learn? We learned about data types and type conversion, how to write and call functions and methods. We also learned how to write code by writing code! It's the best way to learn any programming language. On our journey, we ended up learning how to write a weather app three different ways: As a standalone GUI, a command line app, and finally a web-based application that we deployed to the web! Not bad for just starting out!

We also learned how to deploy code to an online repository called GitHub, a good skill to know if you're planning a career as a programmer.

Beyond just writing a few scripts, we also covered the basics of Object-Oriented Programming, a programming paradigm that relies on the concept of classes and objects. In that discussion, we talked about how derived classes have an "is a" relationship with their parent classes and that composite classes have a "has a" relationship. (A car *is a* vehicle, and it *has a* motor.)

We went over common programming errors, how to diagnose and treat them, and how to perform systematic troubleshooting strategies.

Chapter 7 was dedicated solely to the task of creating a web-based weather app. That's where we wrote a command-line version of the app and used that to build our web-based one.

After that, we looked at data analysis and visualization and we saw how by turning our numbers into visual representations we can better convey our data's story.

Then we dove into scripting and automation with several hands-on scripts. There again, we only scratched the surface, but you have a good foundation to build on.

Finally, we covered database basics and Python integration where we learned how to connect Python to a database and wrote an app to interact with one. We also learned some basic SQL concepts and commands.

While this is the end of this book, don't let this be the end of your Python journey! Challenge yourself and think of ways you can use Python to automate tasks, solve problems, and even enhance your career!

Please Leave Me a Review!

If you enjoyed what you learned from this book, please take a few moments to leave a review. As an independent author with a small marketing budget, reviews are my livelihood on this platform. If you enjoyed this book, I'd really appreciate your honest feedback. I would love to hear from you, and I personally read every review.

https://www.amazon.com/dp/B0CRS9HJC7

Follow Me!

You can follow and message me on Facebook page *Nontechnically Speak* at: https://www.facebook.com/ntspeak

You can also follow me on Instagram at
https://www.instagram.com/htack210/

API: Application Programming Interface. These are common throughout the coding world. Most software programs will have an API which is a set of rules that allow your code to interact with a given application. For example, ChatGPT has an API that allows you to incorporate its AI with your web page to provide human-like responses to user questions.

Boolean: A data type with a true or false setting. You'll see Booleans used in conditional statements. The data type is named for 19th-century English mathematician George Boole and is pronounced: /ˈboolēən/. When written, it is supposed to be capitalized since it is a proper noun.

Decorator: A function that modifies other functions or methods.

Data Science: "Data science combines math and statistics, specialized programming, advanced analytics, artificial intelligence (AI), and machine learning with specific subject matter expertise to uncover actionable insights hidden in an organization's data. These insights can be used to guide decision-making and strategic planning." (What Is Data Science? | IBM, n.d.)

Dunder Methods: A way to use operator overloading in Python (e.g., `__init__`).

Function: A module of code that performs a specific task.

Git: This is a version control system for tracking changes in your code. If you are experimenting with a new feature, you can create a separate branch of your code just for that feature, and later merge it into your main code once you're satisfied the new feature is stable. It's also helpful if you are collaborating on a project with other developers. Each of you can work on your own branch of the main code and work on your portion of the project. You can then review each other's work and decide what should be merged into the main project.

Indentation Error: A mistake in indentation that leads to coding errors. These are errors in syntax rather than logic. Python is particular about its coding structure and uses indentation to enforce its syntax rules. When something is not formatted correctly, it will throw an error because the syntax is how it understands what you are trying to do. Seems harsh, I know. It's kind of like that high school English teacher who's keeping you from graduating because you used a comma splice once. It's a pain in the neck, but you have to respect the syntax!

Iteration (iterating, iterative): " Iteration, in the context of computer programming, is a process wherein a set of instructions or structures are repeated in a sequence a specified number of times or until a condition is met. When the first set of instructions is executed again, it is called an iteration. When a sequence of instructions is executed in a repeated manner, it is called a loop." (Rouse, 2011)

Machine Learning: "Machine learning is a branch of artificial intelligence (AI) and computer science which focuses on the use of data and algorithms to imitate the way that humans learn, gradually improving its accuracy." (What Is Machine Learning? | IBM, n.d.)

Module: A mode is a file that contains Python code that can be used by other programs. For example, if your code is designed to print something, rather than writing your code to print a file, you can use a Python printer module instead.

Numpy: A scientific computing and numerical operations library for Python.

Parameter: A variable that is used by a function as an input to complete a task. For example, the print() function takes a String parameter. It uses that parameter to output the string it was given and show it on the screen.

PEP 8: A style guide for writing Python code that is clear and readable. The guide is not written in stone. If your syntax is acceptable to Python, it will work, but code written in the style as laid out by PEP is best practice.

Pipenv: A Python package manager that manages dependencies and simplifies the use of libraries and dependencies for Python projects.

Procedural Programming: "Procedural programming is a programming paradigm built around the idea that programs are sequences of instructions to be executed. They focus heavily on splitting up programs into named sets of instructions called procedures, analogous to functions. A procedure can store local data that is not accessible from outside the procedure's scope and can also access and modify global data variables." (DeepSource | the Modern Static Analysis Platform, n.d.)

Psuedo Code: "Pseudocode is a detailed yet readable description of what a computer program or algorithm should do. It is written in a formal yet readable style that uses a natural syntax and formatting so it can be easily understood by programmers and others involved in the development process." (Sheldon, 2023)

Pythonic: Adherence to Python's coding style and best practices. Writing code in a way that follows Python conventions and guidelines.

Scientific Computing: "Computational science, also known as scientific computing, technical computing or scientific computation (SC), is a division of science that uses advanced computing capabilities to understand and solve complex physical problems." (Wikipedia contributors, 2023)

Syntax Sugar: Shortcuts in syntax that make code easier to read and write. You'll often see this kind of syntax with common operations. You can think of it as a kind of coding shorthand.

Variable: A variable is a value that can change. They are passed to methods and functions to be acted upon. Think of a variable as a kind of labeled container for storing data but the box can only contain one kind of data. For example, if that variable is of type string, the box can only contain strings, not numbers, integers, or any other kind of thing, only strings.

Virtual Environment: Isolated Python environments for managing project-specific dependencies.

  - *Explanation:* Prevents conflicts between project dependencies and keeps your projects self-contained.

Web Scraping: This is the practice of extracting data from websites using code. This is useful for things like data analysis from websites.

Chapter One

Add 2 Numbers

```
1    # Practice Exercise 1: Calculate the Sum of Two Numbers
2    num1 = float(7)
3    num2 = float(3)
4    #Extra: Comment out lines 2 and 3 and substitute these:
5    # num1 = float(input('What is your first number? '))
6    # num2 = float(input('What is your second number? '))
7    result = (num1 + num2)
8    print(str(num1) + ' + ' + str(num2) + ' = ' + str(result)) # 7.0 + 3.0 = 10.0
```

Manipulate a String

```
1    # Practice Exercise 2: String Manipulation
2    sentence = "The quick brown fox jumped over the lazy dog."
3    #Comment out line 2 and use line 4 instead
4    # sentence = input("Enter a sentence: ")
5    length = len(sentence)
6    uppercase_sentence = sentence.upper()
7    print("Length of the sentence:", length) #Length 45
8    print("Uppercase sentence:", uppercase_sentence)
9
```

Concatenate Strings to Make a Greeting

```
1    # Practice Exercise 3: String Concatenation and Greeting Message
2    first_name = "Ima"
3    last_name = "Nerd"
4    #Extra: Comment out lines 2 and 3 and use lines 5 and 6 instead.
5    # first_name = input("Enter your first name: ")
6    # last_name = input("Enter your last name: ")
7    full_name = first_name + " " + last_name
8    greeting = "Hello, " + full_name + ". Welcome to Python!"
9    print(greeting)
10
```

Chapter Two

Walk the Dog

```
1    # Walk the dog
2    condition = input('What\'s the condition outside? ' )
3    weather = ['sunny', 'cloudy', 'rainy']
4
5    if condition in weather:
6        if condition == 'cloudy' or condition == 'sunny':
7            print('It\'s okay to walk the dog because it\'s ' + condition + ' out.')
8        else:
9            print('We\'re staying in because it\'s ' + condition + ' out.')
10   else:
11       print('We ain\'t going nowhere! It\'s unicorn weather outside!')
```

Shopping Help

```
1    # Iterating through a list
2    shopping_list = ['milk','eggs','bacon','coldcuts','bananas']
3    dairy = ['milk','yogurt','cheese','ice cream','butter']
4    meat = ['beef','pork','bacon','coldcuts']
5    fruit = ['apples', 'bananas', 'oranges']
6
7    for item in shopping_list:
8        if item in dairy:
9            print(item + ' is in dairy.')
10       elif item in meat:
11           print(item + ' is in meats.')
12       elif item in fruit:
13           print(item + ' is in produce.')
14       else:
15           print('Can\'t find ' + item +'? Ask somebody!')
```

Link to all completed code in this book

http://tinyurl.com/KEY4P

When you click on the files in these folders, you'll probably get a preview

error. This is normal. Just download the files and view them in your IDE.

REFERENCES

Blog. (2023, May 5). IT Automation with Python.

https://www.advsyscon.com/blog/it-automation-with-python/

CrowdStrike. (2023, May 17). What is CRUD? Create, read, update, and delete - CrowdStrike. crowdstrike.com.

https://www.crowdstrike.com/cybersecurity-101/observability/crud/

DeepSource | The Modern Static Analysis Platform. (n.d.).

https://deepsource.com/glossary/procedural-programming

Deery, M. (2023, August 30). The Flask Web Framework: A Beginner's Guide. CareerFoundry.

https://careerfoundry.com/en/blog/web-development/what-is-flask/

Doherty, E. (n.d.). What is object-oriented programming? OOP explained in depth. Educative.

https://www.educative.io/blog/object-oriented-programming#what-is-oop

General Python FAQ. (n.d.). Python Documentation.

https://docs.python.org/3/faq/general.html

Old, V. I. N. (2023, November 9). Why are game glitches called bugs?

https://www.vintageisthenewold.com/game-pedia/why-are-game-glitches-called-bugs

OpenAI. (2023). Key Differences Between dropna() and fillna(0) in
Pandas. OpenAI Documentation.
https://www.openai.com/documentation/

Python Double Slash (//) Operator: Floor Division – LearnDataSCI. (n.d.).
https://www.learndatasci.com/solutions/python-double-slash-
operator-floor-
division/#:~:text=In%20Python%2C%20we%20can%20perform,f
loor()%20function.

Python - Functions. (n.d.).
https://www.tutorialspoint.com/python/python_functions.htm

Python, R. (2023, June 16). Inheritance and Composition: A Python OOP
guide. https://realpython.com/inheritance-composition-
python/#whats-inheritance

Real Python. (2022, January 6). Creating a simple Python web
application with Flask and testing locally [Video]. YouTube.
https://www.youtube.com/watch?v=Aa-F6zqLmig

Rouse, A. P. B. M. (2011, August 18). What is Iteration? - Definition from
Techopedia. Techopedia.
https://www.techopedia.com/definition/3821/iteration

Sheldon, R. (2023). pseudocode. WhatIs.com.
https://www.techtarget.com/whatis/definition/pseudocode

Singh, V., & Singh, V. (2023). Difference between methods and functions
in Python. Shiksha Online. https://www.shiksha.com/online-

courses/articles/difference-between-methods-and-functions-in-python/

What is a database? (n.d.). https://www.oracle.com/database/what-is-database/

What is Data Science? | IBM. (n.d.). https://www.ibm.com/topics/data-science

What is Machine Learning? | IBM. (n.d.).

https://www.ibm.com/topics/machine-learning

Wiki, C. T. P. (n.d.). Monokerophobia. Phobia Wiki.

https://phobia.fandom.com/wiki/Monokerophobia

Wikipedia contributors. (2023). Computational science. Wikipedia.

https://en.wikipedia.org/wiki/Computational_science

Glenn Haertlein has worked in the tech sector for over 20 years. He has been a Java developer, a SQL developer, a business analyst, and an application support analyst to name a few things. He currently works as an IS consultant for an international IS consultancy firm. Throughout his career, he has also been involved with writing training documentation for technical and non-technical audiences. Over the years he has learned whether the audience is tech-savvy or not, at the end of the day, both want the same thing: They just want to know how to use software to get things done, and this is what makes his writing, clear, down-to-earth and approachable.